# Dancing in Thin Air

*"When you walk on thin ice, you might as well dance".*
— *Kate Rogers*
*from the poem "Water" in* Passages

# DANCING IN THIN AIR

LOOKING BACK ON SIXTY YEARS OF DANCE AT THE BANFF CENTRE

BRIAN MACDONALD

THE BANFF CENTRE
PRESS

Library and Archives Canada Cataloguing in Publication

Macdonald, Brian, 1928-
        Dancing in thin air : looking back on sixty years of dance at the Banff Centre / Brian Macdonald ; editor, Carol Anderson.

Includes bibliographical references.
ISBN 978-1-894773-29-4

        1. Banff Centre.  Dance Dept.--History.  2. Dance schools--Alberta--Banff--History.  I. Anderson, Carol, 1951-  II. Title.

GV1788.6.B36M33 2007      j792.8'071'0713541      C2007-903170-6

Edited by Carol Anderson
Copy edited by Lesley Cameron
Cover and Book design Tania Craan
Printed and bound in Canada by Houghton Boston

Photos from 1990 to the present were taken by The Banff Centre photographer, Don Lee, and his assistants.

Additional photography credits:
Page 18: Whyte Museum of the Canadian Rockies (V180/III.A.ix.17/Ron Duke)
Page 19: photographer Lori Larson
Page 22: Whyte Museum of the Canadian Rockies (V180/II.A.iii.43)
Page 23: Whyte Museum of the Canadian Rockies (V180/II.A.ix.14/Cascade Cameras)
Page 51 and 69: photographer Ed Ellis
Page 100: Les Grands Ballets Canadiens, photographer Andrew Oxenham
Page 128: photographer Ron Diamond

*Symphony in C* © The School of American Ballet

The Banff Centre Press
107 Tunnel Mountain Dr.
Box 1020
Banff, AB
T1L 1H5
http://www.banffcentre.ca/press/

A thank you goes to the Alberta Foundation for the Arts for their generous support of this project.

This book is dedicated to the dancers, teachers, musicians and staff of The Banff Centre and most especially to ballerina Annette av Paul with gratitude for their devotion to the ideal of *inspiring creativity*.

# TABLE OF CONTENTS

The mountains that surround us in the Bow Valley, I've always felt, bespeak the fragility of human existence, and doubly emphasize the evanescence of dance. Of all the arts, ours is born of sweat, rhythm, and space. Living only for the slightest fraction of time, dance evolves tenuously, flickering like a butterfly on a faraway peak, caught between earth and sky. So do we dancers also exist, letting the wind possess us, fortunate to be airborne and yet still to be on earth.

# Introduction

THE EXCITEMENT OF undertaking this volume of photos and reminiscences of the dance program at The Banff Centre provoked a flood of half-forgotten memories of incidents, plans, meetings, rehearsals, teachers, storms and sunsets, and, of course, dancers. At a rough estimate, somewhere between three and four thousand of them must have graced the Centre's various studios and stages since the program's beginnings in 1947. Our pages were therefore in danger of being overcrowded with multitudes of half-remembered faces and physiques, classes, performances, hopes, and decisions.

I started interviewing across Canada to hear what memories lingered in those who had moved on to different territories or professions, or who had simply retired. After some fifty tapings, I reflected on the results of all the questioning, and found to my surprise that "I had the time of my life" or "the best summer I can ever remember" formed a consistent chorus of flashbacks. I genuinely hadn't expected that result but it persuaded me to cull the unexpected unanimity and to drop into the text some of the individual and pithy comments. They are, I hope, revealing.

I should mention, too, that when I or any Canadian dancer refer to Banff, we don't mean the picturesque town nestled in the Bow River Valley, or even The Banff Centre on the side of Tunnel Mountain. Nor is it a generic term for all the activities of the Centre and its logo "Inspiring Creativity"! In dancer lingo "Banff" simply means the Dance Department, which has functioned now every year for some sixty years. It is a program sustained by young blood, eager muscles, grace, and the need to train in the embrace of an art as old as humanity and almost as old as the surrounding mountains.

I hope that the various abbreviations are not confusing. For as long as I can remember RWB has meant the Royal Winnipeg Ballet, RAD the Royal Academy of Dancing, LGBC Les Grands Ballets Canadiens, NBC the National Ballet of Canada, ESDQ the École Supérieure de Danse de Québec, and among later companies ABC simply the Alberta Ballet Company, and BBC Ballet British Columbia.

I have named only a few specific dancers. A particular few, especially those of whom there are good photos and whose careers were influenced by the Banff experience, pop up from various decades. The photos herein have come from a variety of sources. Some are old and grainy but tell the story nevertheless. Some come from our archives, now well maintained, and others are from dancers' scrapbooks. I particularly wish more photos had been found of the early years. With what were available, we have tried to show the beginnings and the progress of both the program and the succeeding generations of participants.

Over the years there have been distinguished teachers in abundance, a plethora of young choreographers, many devoted pianists, and an army of stage crew and managers, contributors all. David Leighton, Carol Phillips, Paul Fleck, Graeme Macdonald, and Mary Hofstetter have all maintained unwavering stewardship of the vision of the late Senator Donald Cameron, who, in the program's formative years, set out an extraordinary path for us to follow.

Marylu Moyer, from the Stratford Festival, became a devoted archivist in my office in Stratford, matching names to dates, clippings to programs, and faces to photos with patience and sympathy.

Carol Anderson, editor, brought much appreciated expertise and authority in all areas of both dance and text. The cover and text design were the art of Tania Craan and greatly appreciated. Without their professional help and that of the many dancers who reminisced so readily much of the story would not have been untangled.

In the theatrical tradition of presenting flowers in tribute I would add bouquets to Janet Amy and Jane Parkinson who have sought out many of the photos and photographer Don Lee who relentlessly tried to catch our best moments. In the past, theatre manager Bill Pappas and super-coordinator George Ross patiently tilled the garden of our growth and the wonderful team of David LaHay, Susan Toumine and many other teachers chose the young cuttings every spring, nourished them very carefully and watched them bloom. My wife, ballerina Annette av Paul, gardener extraordinaire, greatly cultivated succeeding years of young hopefuls and helped our mountain valley to flower, continuing the vision of Gweneth Lloyd, Betty Farrally, and Arnold Spohr.

# Foreword

## Dance in Banff is Sixty Years Old!

Anniversaries are important. They remind us of the foundations upon which today's accomplishments are built — the individuals, the effort, the programs, and particularly the commitments and values that have brought us to the present day.

This volume is a tribute to the sixty years of history underpinning the Dance Program at The Banff Centre. It is also a reminder of the key role that this institution and its staff have played in the international success that Canadian dancers and dance companies enjoy in the world today. And it underlines the fact that this success has been built across the country, from east to west, from small communities to large, from volunteers to professionals at all levels.

The story takes place in the fairy-tale setting of Banff and The Banff Centre, a mountain retreat dedicated to the arts and artists, where painters rub shoulders with musicians, composers with actors, dancers with writers and set designers — a haven for all the arts, which itself will celebrate its 75th anniversary in 2008.

The dance story at Banff is one of growth and development, from humble western Canadian beginnings and aspiring beginners to a range of programs covering all stages of a dance career, culminating in professional training and performances of the highest level, taught by some of the dance world's leading instructors.

To write this history with knowledge and insight requires a special individual and there is no better author/historian than Brian Macdonald, whose long and varied involvement at Banff, and whose distinguished international career as choreographer, stage director, dancer, and teacher, is without parallel in Canada today. He has *lived* much of this history, and knows whereof he writes. It is a remarkable story, told by a remarkable man.

David Leighton
President, The Banff Centre (1970-83)

When she came to Canada, Gweneth Lloyd brought with her a pioneering spirit that was to have a huge impact on dance, particularly throughout the western provinces. Gweneth did everything. She taught classes and was a Royal Academy and Cecchetti examiner, she choreographed extensively, and founded schools; the Royal Winnipeg Ballet, our dance program at Banff, etc. I used to call her Mother Superior (although only after she had had a gin and tonic). In truth I meant she was a mother of dance in Canada, trimming skirts one moment, teaching constantly, encouraging us all, and receiving an honorary degree with a twinkle in her eye. She is seen here with Senator Cameron in 1968.

# Gweneth and the Senator

The Studio
Room 705
333 Portage Ave
Winnipeg, Man.
January 31, 1941

To Donald Cameron

I understand that in the past you have had movement or dancing in the curriculum of your summer school at Banff, and, in the event of you not having engaged an instructor for this subject, I wondered if you would consider my application.

I am qualified to teach ballet dancing, natural expressive movement, national dancing and mime, having received my training in London, living and teaching there for 10 years before coming to Canada in 1938...

Gweneth Lloyd

4th February, 1941

To Gweneth Lloyd

... As our staff is pretty well completed for this year, I am afraid we will not be able to make use of your services. We shall be glad to keep your name in mind in case we have an opening another year.

Donald Cameron

December 12, 1946
Miss Gweneth Lloyd
The Canadian School of Ballet
491 Main Street
Winnipeg, Man.

To Gweneth Lloyd

... On going into the matter of the programme for our Drama Division in the 1947 Banff School of Fine Arts, we have decided that it would be desirable to make a start on the Ballet this year with a junior instructor. When I was in Winnipeg I believe that you mentioned that a Jean Sterling, one of your students, might fill this position satisfactorily. We would be prepared to pay Miss Sterling $250.00 inclusive of salary, transportation and subsistence for her services.

June 12th, 1947

To Mr. Cameron

We are busy working on the syllabus but are rather held up until you can tell us how many of the students are enrolled for the ballet only and how many in relation to the drama...Is there any chance of your needing one of my girls to help in the domestic line, she is very efficient in that line as in her dancing, but badly needs a job for the summer while we are closed.

June 18, 1947

To Gweneth Lloyd

... It should be possible for Ballet classes to be carried on at any time of the day. So far there are 9 registrations for Ballet only and 16 for Ballet and some other subject (mostly Theatre).

I am rather keen to do some work in the open air and there is an excellent site for an open air theatre near where the future school is to be built on the side of Tunnel Mountain. If it is at all possible I will have an area levelled which would be suitable for both actors and dancers. It was in this connection that I was thinking of the "Trojan Women" or "Medea."

R.H.G Orchard
Ass't Prof. Drama.

November 12th, 1947

To Gweneth Lloyd,

... We are now in the process of making plans for the 1948 Banff School of Fine Arts which will be held from July 13th to August 21st inclusive. The Ballet was such a success last year that we want to continue it, and I am wondering whether or not you would be prepared to come yourself this year, or would you send Miss Stirling (sic) again. I must say she was quite satisfactory.

November 17th, 1947

To Donald Cameron,

... I should very much like to come myself this year, but before I let you know definitely I should be glad if you would tell me what salary you are able to offer, as of course I should not consider coming for the same as Miss Stirling (sic). I should tell you Miss Stirling is no longer on my staff. She is teaching ballroom dancing at the local Arthur Murray school!

Are you expecting the course to be larger this year and if so are you intending to make it a separate course yet?

10th December 1947

Dear Miss Lloyd

I saw Mr. Cameron yesterday (in the hospital)...he was thinking of offering you $325.00 to cover transportation, subsistence and salary, an inclusive fee.

A.N., office secretary

Dear Miss Nelson,

I am afraid that the salary offered by Mr. Cameron is far below the fee which I usually receive for similar work. Taking into account my experience and position in the dancing world I would not be able to accept a position on the staff for less than $600.00 as an inclusive fee.

18th December 1947

Dear Miss Lloyd

Mr. Cameron feels that if he has to engage a pianist in addition to paying your fee, the cost would be too great. If arrangements cannot be made for you to come, Mr. Cameron would like to have Jean McKenzie. Before writing to her, however, he would like to hear from you again.

A.N., office secretary

December 19th, 1947

Dear Miss Nelson,

I think the best plan will be for Miss McKenzie to do the course. I shall of course supervise the syllabus and am very sorry that I shall not be there, but, in any case, shall be better off the following year in my work after I have been able to stay longer refreshing my ideas in England. I hope Mr. Cameron is feeling better and that the School will be even more of a success than last year.

One of the best investments the school ever made was to persuade Gweneth Lloyd of the famed Royal Winnipeg Ballet to head the infant Ballet Division at The Banff Centre. Thus began a 20-year love affair between Miss Lloyd and the Ballet School which was to last until she retired in 1968 after building the Ballet School to the largest in America. Gweneth Lloyd was so popular in her first year that every member of the Drama and Eurythmics Section wanted to take her courses and she had a registration of 80.

from *The Impossible Dream*
(Senator Donald Cameron,
August 1977)

It has been impossible to find any further correspondence between the hard-bargaining Cameron and the canny Lloyd on the subject of her fee, but I imagine he paid the demanded $600, persuaded himself it was a sound investment, and was delighted with the result! They enjoyed a very cordial relationship for over twenty years. She was as canny as he was, and he could be as generous as she.

Once in the early 1960s, Gweneth left me to negotiate my fee for a summer's teaching and choreographing directly with the unpredictable Scot himself. I calculated carefully, having been taught by my Scottish father to lace requests for money with extreme polite-ness, and began by saying, "Well, sir, being now a widower and having to rely on the odd TV job for income, I have to scramble to keep the bills paid and young Brian in private school, which comes to $1500 a year, and I just don't know how I can keep working as a choreographer unless I can earn that much every summer, and I love the Banff school (there was Tchaikovsky, I'm sure, playing in the background) but I don't know if..." Before I could get in another word Cameron said, "Fine. Fifteen-hundred, eh? Then that's your fee. Make sure you get here on time and bring that boy with you, we need more youngsters around!"

Is it any wonder I'm still here?

# Gweneth

SOMEWHERE IN THE VARIOUS accounts of Gweneth and Betty's decision to move from England to Canada (in 1938) is buried a reference to the fact that once upon a time in Gweneth's schooling in the thirties there was a gymnastics teacher who had been born in Canada but who was teaching in England. Thus, some years later, Gweneth, by now an accredited Royal Academy teacher, was invited on a summer holiday to visit her old teacher in her native Winnipeg. Imagine! Winnipeg in 1937, late in the Great Depression. Motley mid-continental Winnipeg. Whatever the impression made on the already experienced teacher, keen, along with Betty Farrally, for a change it became decisive in their plans to settle

abroad and start a new school. Not Auckland, Sydney, Singapore, New Delhi, Cape Town, Toronto, or anywhere else in the Empire. In Winnipeg! I can imagine Gweneth telling Betty, "I've been there. It's a jolly spot. I'm sure they'll welcome a new school. Let's try." The results (the Royal Winnipeg Ballet, The Canadian School of Ballet, the Kelowna Ballet, the Alberta Ballet, and Ballet British Columbia) became part of our cultural history. What happened at The Banff Centre was singular.

It is doubtful that these are all dance students. More than likely they are drama students, perhaps coaxed into second arabesque by the imperious Miss McKenzie. As we see clearly sixty years later our beginnings were modest, but always very well intentioned.

20

The early days of dance at The Banff Centre are typified by these photos. Jean McKenzie, star of the young Winnipeg Ballet, is supposedly warming up here, helped by two actors on the set of the play *School for Husbands*. The plethora of props surrounding the stretching dancer suggests artful posing, and not the workspace of the dance studio. There is little suggestion of what the Dance Program will become later in the twentieth century.

Eva von Gencsy teaching a group of Banff children in 1953.

As early as 1954, Eva von Gencsy is listed in a Banff program as dancing and teaching with Gweneth Lloyd and Betty Farrally, just one of the many roles she plays in the history of dance in Canada. Trained in Hungary, she came to Canada after the war, became a principal dancer with the Royal Winnipeg Ballet and later danced for many years, again as a principal dancer, with Les Grands Ballets Canadiens. She was an amazingly versatile performer in roles as diverse as Lou in *The Shooting of Dan McGrew* and Odette-Odile in *Swan Lake*. She became interested in jazz, both as a performer and teacher, danced in hundreds of television shows and became known internationally for her jazz classes. She is glamorous and unfailingly positive towards her students, and today still teaches with amazing energy and love of dance. Eva is a treasure.

Betty Davis, a teacher and examiner from England's Royal Academy
of Dance, is seen here training teachers. Such training was a vital
step in helping to create awareness of a pedagogical system that
was an enormous impetus to the growth of dance in Canada.
These photos reveal a great deal about our beginnings.

In 1960, Gweneth, Betty, and I looked like this. An unlikely trio, we each had our strengths, shared our weaknesses and managed an enormously dynamic Dance Department. Gweneth retired in 1967. Betty stayed on until her death in 1988 to run the department with Brydon Paige and me. Now Annette av Paul and David LaHay continue the traditions of careful training, well-calculated and polished performances, and a pervasive love of dance. Continuity protects the program's idealism and the nourishing quality of the teaching.

This grainy snapshot holds a secret. Although all who enter Banff National Park are expressly forbidden to feed the animals, be they deer, elk, moose, or bear, a certain individual felt such regulations simply did not pertain to her. She kept a trunkful of food in her car for all the animals, all the time. Thus the only person who could be blithely feeding a bear from the window of her car (circa 1960) must be ... Betty!

All her life, Betty Hey Farrally was a spark plug. Actually, multiple spark plugs. Disdaining her family's plans for her, she studied classical ballet in England with Gweneth Lloyd and obtained her Royal Academy of Dancing credentials to perform, teach, and become an examiner. She did not have a good body for classical line and movement, but she had unstoppable willpower. She joined Gweneth in starting several schools in England and, when the two of them grew restless and decided to move on, they chose and descended on unlikely Winnipeg. The results were not as unexpected as one might think. Tirelessly, they established a school and created opportunities, starting a Sunday Ballet Club, obtaining a royal charter, and eventually developing an internationally honoured company. Gweneth choreographed constantly, but it was Betty who marshalled the forces, and who had the instincts and the drive to inspire performers. She had an animal's eyes, quick, wary, and, if need be, foxy.

Later, when the indomitable duo had resettled in Kelowna where they brought their Canadian School of Ballet, the widow Farrally turned her energies onto an unlikely venue, as possibilities materialized at the mountainside arts centre in Banff. She was by this time a motherly midwife who could terrorize dancers in class or rehearsal, and then bundle as many as would fit into her car off to the hot springs to ease the day's aches and pains. During the winter months she taught up and down British Columbia, rehearsing performances and preparing students for Royal Academy exams. In the summer at Banff she kept both junior and senior programs fuelled and running smoothly. She supported Gweneth in every way as a partner in the everlasting duty of training and encouraging young dancers. Tiny, she had to stand on a chair to see everyone properly in a big rehearsal, and from there dispensed the wit and wisdom that many young dancers would remember for the rest of their lives.

Early in our dance history, we offered classes for the very young, who usually came from the town of Banff or were offspring of the staff. These classes lasted only a few years, for we soon began admitting young dancers only at the elementary level, gradually adding courses for teachers and members of the Royal Winnipeg Ballet. Seen here in a rare 1960 photo is a group of little ones with

David and Anna Marie Holmes, both trained in Vancouver, came to Banff early in their careers, joined the Royal Winnipeg Ballet, went on to Festival Ballet in England, and then to the Dutch National Ballet. *Prothalamion*, a pas de deux I created for them originally for CBC TV in Montreal, became a touchstone for them, especially when they later studied in Leningrad and danced it with the Kirov Ballet on the famous Mariinski stage. They loved spectacular high lifts. David was very strong and had especially accurate timing, and Anna Marie was fearless. I seem to remember that this photo was taken on the roof of Donald Cameron Hall.

This scene is not what it might initially appear to be! It is probably
the finale of *Pleasure Cruise*, one of the many ballets by Gweneth
Lloyd that sustained The Banff Centre's Dance Program during the
twenty years she directed it. Virtue and cruising are an unlikely
combination and only possible on a very small stage (in what has
now become a tourist information centre!). The Dance Program's
beginnings did indeed make for strange bedfellows.

"Banff propelled me into a career when I was
not even eighteen years old." — C.G.

This 1961 photo of Gweneth Lloyd's *Arabesque* includes Stephanie
Finch, Karen Fawcett, Gina Hiscock, Donna Kirkbride, Sharon
McBurney, Shirley New, Janet Paterson, Jennifer Penney, Lydia
Watt, and Sharon Kirk. The thin little youngster second from the
left is Jennifer Penney, a student of Gweneth and Betty's who was
picked to go to the Royal Ballet School. She later joined the Royal
Ballet where she became a principal dancer and a muse of Kenneth
MacMillan's, creating roles in several of his most successful ballets.
The young man in the centre is Richard Cragun, who became an
extraordinary principal dancer and had a worldwide career with
the Stuttgart Ballet.

Gweneth's *Finishing School* was perhaps inspired by Lichine's *Graduation Ball*, but bore only a slight resemblance to the earlier work. It was one of many ballets she choreographed for the Royal Winnipeg Ballet and the Banff Dance Program. First composing her ballets on paper and then teaching her choreography to the dancers, she was quite able to picture the outcome of her dances before a single rehearsal. Seen here are Sheila Molloy and Shirley New, who realized early her ambition to join the Royal Winnipeg Ballet after studying with Ruth Carse, another Alberta dance pioneer, and later danced with Les Grands Ballets Canadiens. Also pictured is Bill Lark who, after this picture was taken, went on to serve in the US Air Force in Vietnam, and later joined the Royal Winnipeg Ballet, danced with a number of companies in Europe and subsequently taught for many years in Taiwan.

Dancers taking a break from a 1964 rehearsal of *Les Sylphides*, first performed by our dancers in the Banff Community Centre downtown. The young man is Nils-Ake Häggbom, who became a principal dancer and later Artistic Director of the Royal Swedish Ballet. Next to him is Annette av Paul, a principal dancer with the Royal Swedish Ballet and Les Grands Ballets Canadiens and now director of the Summer Dance Program at the Banff Centre. Right of Annette is the young Maureen Eastick, a well-known teacher in Victoria, and one of our most valuable teachers in the Training Program in Banff.

This little tyke, Virginia Wakelyn, seen here with Dalton Davis in 1958, was born in Banff. After she had attended the Summer Dance Program for a couple of years, Gweneth told her parents that their child had genuine talent. She suggested that Virginia be moved to Toronto, where Gweneth was teaching, that she be placed in an academic school, and her progress carefully watched. At age fifteen, Virginia was given special permission to join the Royal Winnipeg Ballet, where she stayed for three and a half years, again spending every summer in the Banff programs. Then she went to the Royal Ballet School, where she was plucked out of class by Dame Ninette de Valois. She joined the Royal Ballet and danced with that company for ten years becoming a soloist, then married, retired, had two sons, and started an enormously successful ballet school, which she just recently sold. Gweneth, Betty, and the Banff programs initiated a life's journey. Look again at the blonde tyke, and marvel at what the prescience of her teachers and Gini's talent achieved.

ANNETTE av PAUL was trained first by her mother and then by Vaganova teachers at the Royal Swedish Opera House where she began at the age of eight. Being in that environment meant class every day after school, dancing in children's productions, passing yearly exams, being a supernumerary in operas whenever needed, singing in children's choruses, watching Bergman direct *The Rake's Progress*, and seemingly living more at the Opera house than at home. While still a senior student she was picked by the Russian choreographer Yuri Grigorovitch to dance the principal role in "The Stone Flower" his first major work to be mounted in the West. After graduating into the Royal Swedish Ballet she was promoted to principal dancer by the age of 21 when she began being assigned all the major classics. She later danced with the Royal Winnipeg Ballet, the Harkness Ballet of New York and several times toured internationally with Dame Margot Fonteyn. Marrying and moving to Canada she danced over a thousand performances with Les Grands Ballet Canadiens before retiring and beginning a new career as a teacher and artistic director.

For DAVID LAHAY figure skating lead to dance training which lead to becoming apprentice with LGBC where he was a principal dancer for nine years ('78-'87). Early on he picked up a B.A. from Trent University and an Honors B.F.A. in Dance from York University. After experience as a ballet master in several Canadian companies and abroad including eight years as pedagogue and co-director of the Dance Department at The Banff Centre he became the founding Artistic Director of Ballet Kelowna, which now performs throughout British Columbia. There he teaches, choreographs, budgets, sews costumes, fund raises, does the accounting and, on occasion, drives the bus. Extremely able and hard-working, he is also, it should be noted, a soldier's son.

British born SUSAN TOUMINE has been living in Montreal since 1969. She trained in Canada with Nesta Toumine at the Classical Ballet School in Ottawa as well is in New York, London, and Cannes.  This back ground included schooling in the RAD, Cecchetti, and Vaganova syllabus leading to a long dancing career with LGBC, and nine years as a soloist. On retirement she taught for sixteen years at the E.S.D.Q. She has been on the staff of the Dance Department of The Banff Centre since 1984 and is also a certified STOTT Pilates Instructor. She is famously quoted as having said, "My job is to inspire. I cannot teach with vinegar."

BRIAN MACDONALD, O.C., Program Director

An original member of the National Ballet of Canada, Brian Macdonald's association with The Banff Centre dates back to 1960. He has been artistic director of the Royal Swedish Ballet, the Harkness Ballet of New York, the Batsheva Company of Israel and Les Grands Ballets Canadiens. Internationally well-known as a choreographer and director of ballet, opera and musical theatre, he has directed a series of Gilbert and Sullivan productions for the Stratford Festival, all of which became television specials. Since 1987, he has mounted new productions for the Royal Winnipeg Ballet, the New York City Opera, the Edinburgh Festival, the Kennedy Centre in Washington, La Scala, the Sydney Opera House, Les Ballets Jazz de Montréal, the Edmonton and Manitoba Operas, the Canadian Opera Company and most recently a new *Petrushka* for the Gothenburg Ballet in Sweden. He recently directed *Madama Butterfly* for Opera de Quebec, *Tosca* for the National Arts Centre and narrated *Peter and the Wolf* with the NAC Orchestra. For the Broadway run of *The Mikado*, he received Tony award nominations both as director and as choreographer. Mr. Macdonald was awarded the Order of Canada in 1967, the Canada Council Molson Award in 1983, the Canada Dance Award and The Banff Centre National Arts Award in 1988. In 2002 he was appointed a Companion of the Order of Canada, and became a Fellow of The Banff Centre.

Teacher Vera Volkova received her early training in St. Petersburg, where she absorbed the principles and syllabus of the great Russian teacher Agripinna Vaganova. Escaping the political turbulence of the 1920s in Russia, she taught in Shanghai and Hong Kong, but soon settled in London, where she counted Margot Fonteyn and Alicia Alonso among her many students. In 1951, she began what turned out to be a long sojourn in Copenhagen with the Royal Danish Ballet. Arnold Spohr saw her there and quickly became an admirer of her methodology and enthusiasm, inviting her to Banff in 1969, 1971, and 1972. This connection cemented a friendship that affected not only the Banff Program but also Arnold's teaching and direction of the Royal Winnipeg School and company. One writer quoted Volkova as saying that under her vulnerable appearance there was a "core of steel." She was a much-loved influence on all who knew her.

What exactly are these three very focussed dancers doing in 1965? A little guesswork would suggest that the internationally esteemed Vera Volkova is helping guests Billy Martin-Viscount and Linda di Bona with the proper grip of the hands for a famous acrobatic lift, long associated with Asaf Messerer's pas de deux *Spring Waters*, a Soviet "number" and crowd-pleaser in many a *divertissement* program. The girl comes rushing toward the boy's right side, and this grip allows her to be lifted high into the air, behind his back. Then she lands, almost in front of him on his left side, and continues to dance. It is an outrageously circus-like trick. Billy had been to the Bolshoi in Moscow where he learned the complete show-stopping duet. Can you tell from this photo that he is confident, Linda is puzzled, and Volkova is determined that there be no accident or injury? "Hasten slowly," she appears to be saying, "and don't try this at home."

This 1965 photo of Nils-Åke and Annette, from either
a photo shoot or a video-taping, was taken in the "big
studio," actually the Roubakine Concert Hall, a vast
improvement over our modest beginnings in a church
hall in the downtown Banff village. High at the back
are the windows of an observation area. We danced
and taught in this hall, until two even larger studios
were eventually created for us up the hill in the Theatre
Complex. This room, brimming with memories, morphed
into a dining room overlooking the Bow Valley, and will
soon disappear as The Banff Centre enlarges yet again.

*By Jupiter!* Choreographer — Jim Clouser

In the sixties James Clouser, then a principal dancer with the RWB, taught and choreographed alongside Gweneth and Betty for several years. When I contacted him in 2007, memories of his time at Banff had faded somewhat.

He did remember, though, that on the famous night in the summer of 1967, when the Eric Harvie Theatre was formally opened, there were very few actual seats, if any, and the distinguished audience were invited to bring chairs from their rooms so that the opening ceremony and inaugural performance could begin! Of his ballet *By Jupiter!* seen above he could remember little. The photo shows a sculptural sense with Jim himself in the middle of his dancers. A trained musician, he wrote the music for many of his ballets; more likely, according to an old program, the above was to a score by Shostakovitch.

This photograph is from 1967. From left to right: Eric Hampton, Eva von Gencsy, Denise O'Brian, Richard Jones, Patricia Ross and James Clouser pose outside the unfinished Eric Harvie Theatre which would become part of a new complex that included two splendid large studios for the Dance Department. Senator Donald Cameron, the driving force of The Banff Centre, was a stubborn and determined prairie son. Under his watchful eye, and thanks to his constant fundraising, we grew.

Scholarships play an important role in all the programs at The Banff Centre, and are especially important for dancers who, given the nature of their training, are young and often needy. By the time dancers are sixteen or eighteen much of their training must be absorbed, and balanced by academic studies. Summer is a fine time for the youngsters to study and make decisions, but they need financial help as well as career advice. In this photo from 1969, Arnold Spohr presents a scholarship to a young dancer who, I'm sure, thirty-eight years later still remembers, wherever the years have led him, his summer at Banff and the help he received.

Agnes de Mille and Aaron Copland onstage after the premiere of *Rodeo* in 1976. Agnes was a wonderful and successful choreographer, tough, relentlessly professional and an original visionary in American theatre. She was also charming, witty, opinionated and an excellent writer. She had persuaded Copland to write for her what would become one of his most popular scores. She could ignite almost any situation in which she found herself! Bilingually! Arnold asked her to let Banff do *Rodeo*. In New York, she grilled me about the program beforehand, pretending nonchalance. When she finally came to Banff she complained about everything, even the mountains! Back in New York when I asked her why, she said "Well, they were pretty but I was expecting the Grand Canyon or at least Mount Rushmore," eyes twinkling. I loved her.

The cowboy on the far right is the young Kelly Robinson, now a very successful opera director.

Arnold Spohr was aware of the Danish Bournonville heritage, and in 1981 arranged for Anette Amand, ex-dancer and *répétitrice* of the Royal Danish Ballet, to teach and rehearse the third scene of *Konservatoriet* to the Banff Summer Dance Program. Classified, when it premiered at the Royal Theatre in Copenhagen on May 6, 1849, as a "Vaudeville ballet," *Konservatoriet* was full of comic situations built around attempts by the director of the Paris Conservatoire to make a "good catch" in the marriage market. It might well have disappeared by the end of the century but for Bournonville's gifts as a choreographer and the revealing *enchaînements* of the famous third scene ballet class. Here was the master's Friday class, as he taught it, derived from his years at the Conservatoire in Paris, where he was a student of the great August Vestris!

Shown clearly was the buoyant musicality, delicate and effortless, of what was to become known as the Bournonville style. Lightness, great clarity of footwork, speed, and fluidity are its characteristics, a vocabulary that seems to match in some magical way the Danish personality. To call it "merry" is to falsify the intensity of the training required to make it seem so. Ease makes it appear weightless, constantly in a major key, and of a very particular time and place.

The jump, from Vestris to Bournonville to the Royal Danish Ballet, where the style and vocabulary were preserved for decades, to Canada, via Arnold's devotion to the Banff program, was a fortunate one. This opportunity exemplified the Dance Program's intention and opened a new window for the participants.

When Brydon Paige taught *Graduation Ball* to the Banff dancers in 1985, it was exact and detailed. He had learned the ballet from the choreographer David Lichine at Les Grands Ballets Canadiens. A romp of waltzes and high jinks, it includes the finishing school girls, of course, handsome heel-snapping cadets, an overzealous general, and a coy school mistress, all frolicking through broad jokes and loveable stereotypes. *Graduation Ball* is clever froth and perfect for young dancers.

*Façade* was an early hit for the Sadler's Wells Ballet (later the Royal Ballet). Edith Sitwell's poetry and William Walton's music came together with the young Frederick Ashton's choreography into a soufflé of British whimsy that was saucy and truly original. Satirizing popular dance styles of the 1920s, Ashton was what the Brits would call "spot on." *Popular Song, Charleston, Debutante Waltz*, and *Polka* were witty and inventive, while *Tango*, in which a professional dancing partner is languidly seducing an innocent debutante in daring orange satin, evoked a wickedly funny situation. The steps were simple, the interplay was everything.

Certain personalities can mark a role in indelibly wonderful ways. Robert Helpmann and Moira Shearer tangoed into my memory for the longest time. Nadia Nerina was straw-hatted and sharp as a hatpin in the polka, with steely footwork and seemingly lightning speed. Even with the assistance of coaching by Alexander Grant, our Banff dancers couldn't manage the essential Britishness of the choreography or the impish wit. But by staging *Les Patineurs* one season and *Les Rendezvous* the next, as well as *Façade*, we were touched by Ashton's particular style. The dancers loved performing these ballets, although any real success seemed elusive.

*Lignes et Pointes* had been part of a Grands Ballet Canadiens
program dedicated to the Quebec composer Pierre Mercure who
was also a television producer responsible for a great deal of dance
activity in the early years of that medium in Montreal. Brydon Paige
and I each choreographed short sections of the dense and intense
orchestral poem and together managed to create a vivid interpreta-
tion of a *plus-que-moderne* minor masterpiece ... by creating two
pas de deux that only connected at the very last minute.

A predominantly Tchaikovsky program in 1990 included *Valse d'Occasion* and *Serenade*, as well as the Polonaise and Blue Bird excerpts from *Sleeping Beauty*. Here, Mia Allegra Lillard and William Marie appear in one of the most famous moments from the Act III grand pas de deux. Allegra is now retired and directing her own school. William received his first several years' training from Susan Toumine at the École Supérieure in Montreal. An extraordinarily talented dancer, he spent two summers in the Banff program before joining the National Ballet. Tragically, he was killed in a motorcycle accident in New York City in November 2000.

# Week by Week

IMAGINE, IF YOU WILL, just short of 100 dancers moving purposefully about the grounds and buildings of The Banff Centre, youngsters exuberant and more energetic than the young musicians, singers, actors, and theatre technicians with whom they share this sizeable campus on the side of Tunnel Mountain in the Canadian Rockies. They are noisy, as dancers often are outside the strict discipline of the classroom. There are no parents here, and guardians are in evidence only for the very young ones. Several dining rooms assuage the dancers' near-constant hunger. Their days revolve around constant classes and rehearsals, from 9 AM to 9 PM. They move between two theatres, a gym, a pool, and laundry rooms for their sweat-soaked practice clothes.

Experienced teachers hold the reins for these colts. For several weeks every summer The Banff Centre is a focus for dance for a chosen, driven few, and the summer program is an ultimate challenge to embrace and enjoy, a time to cherish. The Training Course, for younger, more elementary students, is five weeks in total with classes in classical ballet, and contemporary and jazz movement, and four performances, in the smaller theatre, of short choreographies suited to their abilities.

The six-week Professional Course is intensive and unique culminating in four public performances. Guest teachers complement the core training offered by the summer staff, while the choreographies learned by the students are as demanding as those that any dancer would encounter in a major professional company. By their late teens, dancers must achieve so much strength, elasticity, line, and musicality that few hours in their young lives can be devoted to other pursuits. At the same time, academic studies are *de rigeur*; many dancers head for university after a performing career, and it is

important that they are fully equipped to do so. Youth however, is the time to acquire the motor skills of dance. To make the body into a whip or a jumping bean, as daring as a high diver, or quick as a cat, requires exceptional dedication. Self-discipline is paramount, bones and sinews must be answerable to a high calling, and the dancer's instrument, once thus honed, has to be that of a superb athlete, possessed of a grace and a dramatic sense that transcend every limit of muscularity.

A youngster, imbued with the art of dance, can often appear to be obsessed by the mirror or perhaps inexplicably gifted, qualities that disguise the exercise and science that they have absorbed over the years. Once a dancer commits to the process of training, it seems never-ending.

## WEEK ONE

Chosen during specially arranged auditions all across Canada, from Halifax to Victoria, or sometimes by video, thirty-six to forty dancers have been accepted into The Banff Centre's Professional Course. Some of them already have paying jobs with companies, others are recent graduates of the major dance schools and are looking for work, while still others have two or three years ahead to complete their academic schooling and training. The dancers' ages range from fifteen to twenty-one, with few exceptions.

On the mid-June morning of the first day of the six-week program, the dancers are gathered in Studio 222 of the Theatre Complex by 8 a.m. Almost always, they are lying on the floor, stretching like lazy animals, working out the kinks from their travel to the mountains. They are gregarious and often bubbling, their apprehensions carefully and deliberately hidden. Some are strangers to one another; others have been in the program

Gioconda Barbuto, seen here with Annette av Paul, first came to Banff as a very young girl, then later as a participant in the Professional Program, and finally, after many years as a soloist with Les Grands Ballets Canadiens, as a Lee Award winner with an international career as a choreographer. We are very proud of her.

before. Newcomers are inclined to be shy and silent. They are all neat and clean, dressed in leotards, tights, and close-fitting T-shirts, their bodies at first hidden in baggy sweatpants and oddly-coloured leg warmers they wear, supposedly to aid the process of warming up. The girls' hair is pulled back and secured in traditional ballet custom. The boys add sweatbands and kerchiefs, venturing a hint of swashbuckle in a traditionally feminine milieu. Scents of perfume and cologne float on the air. As nine o'clock nears, all the dancers stake out places at the barre, either directly by a mirror or carefully avoiding one. Their determination is palpable.

   For the staff, Annette, David, Susie, and me, this moment is a first glimpse into the possibilities of those chosen. In the weeks that follow this June morning they are to become a company, to perform together, to show technique and conviction, to justify their scholarships, to jump forward. So we, the teachers and coaches, move as a group to each dancer along the barre, introducing ourselves, catching names, making mental notes, smiling a lot, not hurrying. When that little ritual is finished I am always careful to announce, "You have passed the audition, a big first step, now enjoy class!" Annette

The spectacular mountain setting has the effect of distancing participants from urban distractions and pressures, leaving them to take full advantage of the resources at hand. There is no other arts workplace and learning-place where the opportunity for development in a professional environment is greater or richer.

— MICHAEL CRABB, *Passages*.

This class-faculty-member shot does have something to say about the Professional Course in 1986. Taken on and in front of the little stage in Roubakine Hall, it includes:

Laura Alonso — daughter of Alicia, and an internationally respected teacher

Brydon Paige — teacher and choreographer

Annette av Paul — recently retired ballerina

Brian Macdonald — choreographer and director of the Summer Dance Program

Betty Farrally — famed teacher and co-founder of the Royal Winnipeg Ballet

Alexander Grant — principal dancer of the Royal Ballet in England and specialist in Ashton ballets

Una Kai — Balanchine teacher and ballet mistress of the Joffrey Ballet

Marquita Lester — head of the Mentor program of Ballet British Columbia

Christopher House — choreographer and winner of the 1986 Lee Award

Earl Stafford — pianist and music director of the Royal Winnipeg Ballet

Members and about-to-be members of the Royal Winnipeg Ballet, the Alberta Ballet and Ballet British Columbia

adds, "There's less oxygen up here in the mountains. You'll get used to it, but if you feel faint, sit down, and don't be ashamed or worry, by the end of the week you'll be breathing like an Olympic runner." David is more pragmatic. He says simply, "Pace yourselves."

In a very few moments sweat will raise the temperature throughout the large space of Studio 222. Class follows a pattern evolved over several hundred years. Barre work, which exercises nearly every muscle from toes to ears, can last up to forty minutes; stretches, often tortuous for tight muscles, follow; next comes centre work, where the process of conquering space perhaps starts with a repeat of some of the barre work but now without support; after this is adagio, which means "at leisure" but is actually a slow, controlled and very linear combination of movements where all effort must be hidden. Pirouettes of several different kinds follow; then faster footwork which means intricate beats, of which there are a multitude; little jumps; and then the BIG jumps in long enough spurts to fully engage the heart and lungs. Repeated 250 to 300 times a year for a good eight years or so, this ritual streamlines the body into grace itself.

Our president, the late Paul Fleck, loved to get into the act. Any act. Here he has arrived onstage for the last pose of *Jeu de Cartes*, originally choreographed for Les Grands Ballets Canadiens, and seen in Banff in 1988.

Kelley McKinlay is typical of the young dancer whose commitment to athletic, artistic rigour, from his teens to adulthood, has earned the admiration of all his teachers. Blessed with musicality and a wonderful high, light jump, Kelley is currently a principal dancer with the Alberta Ballet Company. He is seen here:

As a skinny youngster outside the Max Bell Theatre with Alexis Saunders in 1998.

As a soloist, and with Leigh Allardyce in a performance of *Configurations of the Body* in 2004.

With Courtney Richardson in a performance of *Requiem 9/11* in 2002.

Well, of course, the dancers, on this first day, don't pay attention to us old fogeys and throw themselves into every stretch, turn, and jump with exuberance and no little competitiveness. Suddenly, a new teacher, a new, huge studio, new pianist, and the fresh, mountain air combine into some high-octane dancing and not a little euphoria. Every year it is the same.

Once class is over, it is time for talk. Our co-ordinator joins us and we lay out a few rules of behaviour for rehearsals, injuries, fittings, punctuality, days off, and every detail essential to a professional atmosphere. Annette describes the repertoire to be learned and performed, which ballet is to be newly created, which will be on pointe, the responsibilities of understudying, the daily schedule from studio work to stage time, and how to talk out problems with your teacher or choreographer. She emphasizes other pertinent suggestions: Never, ever be late for a fitting. Ever. Be good to your body. And to each other.

Rob Rubinger was never meant to be a prince in white tights. In fact, in 1989 he was a football-sturdy, cool, funny, likeable dancer who was also dance-wise funky. When we heard that Geneviève Salbaing, a founder of Les Ballets Jazz de Montreal, was coming to see performances in Banff, we quickly strategized. Rob had a short solo in my ballet *Breaks*, easily altered to include a flash of breakdancing. He tossed this off with speed and aplomb, and after the performance was one of three dancers immediately offered a job. He was a mainstay of Les Ballets Jazz for fourteen years, before retiring to join Cirque du Soleil. Q.E.D.

Be polite to your partner. Get lots of sleep. Remember that this is an intensive course. Learn everything you can. And under no circumstances should anyone entertain the idea of white-water rafting or mountain climbing on a day off!

That first afternoon the Lee Award choreographer tries out some new movement and talks about the work to come. Maybe everyone sits on the floor and listens to music, or there is a tentative attempt at partnering, experimental and different, new to the dancers. Watching, we are slyly trying to judge who might look good with whom. Certain dancers have arrived after time off from their company; others were dancing until two days ago. In shape, out of shape, no matter, everyone is going to stiffen up a little, it goes with the territory.

Enthusiasm carries them all through the week although the first Thursday (grumpy Thursday I always call it) finds the boys' arms and shoulders stiff from new lifts and the girls' toes often blistering in their pointe shoes. But there is already momentum; energy and expectations are running high. The food is great, the weekend is coming, and the mountains are awesome.

## WEEK TWO

Although we have said auditions are over, that is not quite true, for as we observe the students we teachers continue to look and question. Who will best perform a leading role? Who will profit most from doing corps work, which is often very challenging? Who has the jump for a particular solo, or who will learn and grow from working on that same solo but may only be a "cover" and perhaps finally not perform the solo? Who presents themselves well and convincingly, and who needs to work on just that? Which boys have

Sarah Murphy-Dyson, from Victoria, and Johnny Wright, from Vancouver, met in the Professional Program, married, and danced with the Alberta Ballet and later with the Royal Winnipeg Ballet, where they both became soloists. Here they are rehearsing *Time Out of Mind* in 1999. They were participants in the Dance Program several times and remain an extraordinary couple, talented, dedicated, and a choreographer's dream.

"Banff taught me that I
could do leading roles!" —J.R.

had a lot of partnering experience — a nice dividend from previous training — and for whom is it a struggle? Who hears the music, really hears it, dances with instinctive musicality, hearing more than just the occasional downbeat? Who arrives early for morning class prancing with energy, and is still exuding that energy come suppertime? Who will, probably, and with any luck, make it into professional ranks, if they are not already there? Who has the drive and stamina for years of dancing? We continue, as teachers, to look and reflect, trusting our own eyes and intuition.

Each one of the staff has responsibilities as a *répétiteur*, preparing and rehearsing a ballet for the performances. We have staff meetings to assure ourselves that the first, tentative casting is indeed the best; in the six weeks we prepare an A cast, a B cast, and a "cover" for every role. ("Everlasting casting" quipped Artistic Director Alexander Grant, who loved epigrams.) This process sometimes includes bargaining …

"If I can have Harry for my first cast, you can have Mary for your third movement. Okay?"

"Couldn't Melissa just cover? She's not that strong yet, is she?"

"Oh, oh, we've left out Bobby! How did that happen? I can use him instead of Philip, who has too much to do anyway."

"If Nicole twists an ankle we're in a terrible mess! She's in everything!"

"May I remind everyone this is not going to premiere at Lincoln Centre! We're in Banff for heaven's sake, it's a learning experience."

"Should we have the nurse keep an eye on Polly? She's looking awfully thin, and she wasn't like that at auditions!"

"Perhaps Roger should be doing light weights twice a week. Maybe more. David, can you start him off at the gym?"

We are like anxious parents. Our youngsters need to be pushed and to push themselves, but always within reason. Parents have trusted us to be wise, so wise we must be, but then again, we're not running a summer camp. As the tempo of classes and rehearsals revs up, we become very aware of how much we can demand and encourage.

The Lee Award choreographer often chooses to work with contemporary movement, trying to invent a new work with a new vocabulary. For this, they inevitably choose, and want to work with, the best classical dancers. Disdaining *pas de bourrées* and *arabesques* as passé, today's choreographers nevertheless frequently rely on centuries-old classical training to create the best instruments for expressing the range and nuance of their movement ideas. The irony of the "old" technique being the best source for the newest moves is all part of a dancer's life now.

This week the casting is nearly finalized. The tempo in the studio quickens. We estimate the number of pointe shoes. CDs of new music are edited. Lists of rehearsal hours are documented and diligently watched. A knowledgeable nutritionist gives an evening lecture and takes questions. Physio appointments start. The lighting chief and assistants sit in rehearsal making notes; lacking words to describe the dancing they start making

Deborah Washington and Claude Caron, shown here in 1990 rehearsing *Breaks*, commissioned by The Banff Centre, with music by Mozart and Freedman. Both dancers are retired now, but not the old man in the sneakers and glasses. Choreographers are like fine wine, supposedly improving with age.

In 1995 Crystal Pite, who originally trained with Maureen Eastick in Victoria, received the Lee Award, after spending several seasons in the Apprentice Program and later in the Professional Program. Seen here in a forest of legs, she is where she always wants to be ... in the studio, surrounded by fellow dancers.

Her summer in Banff led to her joining Ballet British Columbia where she danced for eight years and began choreographing, later joining William Forsythe's company in Frankfurt and then becoming resident choreographer with Les Ballets Jazz in Montreal. She has won many awards and presently performs and creates for her own company, Kidd Pivot, in Vancouver. Her style combines elements of quirky humour, invention, risk, and improvisation.

She is seen here as the Princess in *Firebird*.

diagrams with little stick figures, which will translate into precise cues for the stage manager. Schedules marked "preliminary" or "subject to change" include fittings, extra coaching, more precise measurements, etc. We are still in the second week and projecting calm.

## WEEK THREE

By now we are in high gear. If a work ethic is going to emerge among the tiny, tall, sturdy, pretty, and various other physiques, it becomes particularly clear this week. By the end of morning class, big jumps and all, the rehearsal hall bears a slight resemblance to a sweat lodge; albeit one where a demandingly physical, rather than spiritual, journey takes place, one akin to ceremony. A good teacher is instructive and relentless right to the final *révérance*. Then chocolate bars and oranges are dug out of dance bags, and leg warmers reappear. The occasional boy (usually it's a boy) will slip outside for a cigarette. Everyone drinks copious amounts of water. Everyone freshens up. Some girls, depending on which ballet will be rehearsed first, put new band-aids on their toes and change leotards. Bright colours make a welcome appearance. There are still two hours of rehearsal left before lunch. The boys, who will continue to sweat like stevedores, also change, maybe three times in a day, and smell even more of cologne. Or liniment. Or both. There are occasional jokes and some kidding around, but not much. We have a deadline, the four performances at the end of the sixth week. You are expected to remember well what was accomplished yesterday and a noticeably professional attitude to the day's rehearsal can get you a job. This third week is probably the most demanding; we are all pushing to be much further ahead by the end of it, more than halfway there actually. The Balanchine is completely taught. Victoria Simon, who teaches it, is expert, efficient, quiet-spoken, and infinitely knowledgeable, an anchor of the program. Whichever ballet of mine is to be included is usually roughed through. The Lee Award choreographer, in the throes of creation, always needs "more time please." A program order begins to emerge.

Each summer we prepare either three or four ballets, double-cast. Will cast A and cast B both be strong and interchangeable as hoped? Will understudies and covers get the time needed? Is the wardrobe department happy and busy, or at least not too antsy about casting? Everyone healthy? (The worst that can happen to any dance company is for a cold or flu to get passed around, with sniffles and fevers making a mockery of rehearsal schedules. Celia Franca once said to me, when I complained of what I was dramatically convinced was pneumonia, "Dear boy, you are either rehearsing like everyone else, sitting in a corner watching and taking notes, or home in bed ... take your choice!")

There is another factor, too. It is spring in the young dancers' lives and hormones are on high alert, although there is not much time for socializing. The hot tub is crowded every night with tired bodies in bathing suits that seem to get smaller every year. Oddly, fatigue does not mean misery. Aches and pains are expected. Dancers learn to get on with it. No one ever said ballet was easy, only that it was challenging and fun. It is definitely more fun than basketball or algebra. The dancers all look forward to a Saturday morning run-through to see what has been taught or created so far, a pick-me-up after three weeks of pushing hard.

Usually at this point in the summer the Training Course students arrive, sixty-five to seventy younger dancers, less practised but eager to see everything and start in on their own program. They plunge into classes in ballet, jazz, and contemporary movement and start rehearsing little pieces made specifically for younger bodies, and thus not too rigorous. They bring a huge energy with them and are quickly divided into three groups — the reds, the greens, and the blues. They are carefully supervised; for many of the very young ones it is their first time outside of their home studio and this summer course can often cement their ambitions. They can be a joy to teach or they can drive you crazy. Extra patience becomes the norm, as does encouragement, and when real talent is clearly visible we rejoice with silent hallelujahs. These young dancers are all invited to their elders' rehearsals whenever possible, and are invariably wide-eyed when they watch the older dancers jump, spin, and lift.

For the tenth anniversary of the Professional Program we included Stravinsky's *The Firebird*. We presented a version I had created in 1966 for the Royal Swedish Ballet, which was subsequently danced by the Harkness Ballet of New York and by the Norwegian Ballet. The quintessential Russian fairy tale, *Firebird* was a challenge not only for the dancers but also for all our production and music resources. The costumes, by the Swedish designer Ingve Gamelin, were flown to Banff, the Royal Winnipeg Ballet orchestra's conductor led members of the Calgary Philharmonic, the Alberta Ballet joined us, and the original Russian scenario was respected, although the choreography had some contemporary influences.

In the ballet, a glamourous firebird is captured by a hunting prince. She gives him a feather with which to summon her if attacked in the mysterious forest and flies off, leaving him to discover a shy princess and her attendants playing with golden apples. How's that for symbolism? After the romantic interlude that follows during the night, mysterious monsters emerge, led by the Kostchei, an evil magician, two mischievous bats, and a libidinous snake. At the height of the ensuing confrontation, the prince calls for the firebird. She subdues the forest creatures, and they crawl away. The prince marries the princess in a golden wedding and this archetypal Russian fairy tale finishes with a great chorale.

In Banff, Barbara Moore was the bewitching firebird and Annette, who had created the role of the princess in the original production at the Opera House in Stockholm, taught it to a very young Crystal Pite, who was already showing promise of her incipient international career at that time.

"If you can handle six weeks in the Professional Program, you can handle dancing in a company situation." — C.L.

Special orders of shoes start to arrive. Parts of costumes appear in the rehearsal studio. Everyone looks sleeker. There are always dancers practising at the side of the room after class. There are daily run-throughs of complete ballets. We pick away at details; this is the week to emphasize technique, to be stubborn about it. Next week we start on stage. One of the great privileges of Banff is stage time. Performance schedules are debated, decided, and posted. Who is dancing which night? Cast A or B? Or a combination! Parents are phoned. Plans are made. Everyone becomes very single-minded. Even so, a certain couple are smiling at each other a lot or holding hands on the way to lunch; plus ça change ... the young have their ways.

Every hour of studio time is carefully allotted. With both programs having classes and rehearsals every day we search out extra spaces around the campus. Stage managers and assistants ferry tape recorders and tapes from space to space in a complicated choreography. Pianists cope somehow. As the Centre is situated on the side of a mountain we are all thoroughly oxygenated by now! Schedules are puzzled through and ideally before the day ends are posted all over the campus for the next day. For the professional program, dancers, wardrobe, technical services, wigs, makeup, sound, communications, the front office, the nurse, the entire army must all be marshalled to make the most of every minute. Fittings multiply. Levity comes in short supply. Casting is finally finalized for the final time, absolutely and definitely! The dancing, which will soon move from the studio to the stage, is improving every day. There is more performance quality, more layering, more flow.

On the Saturday of the fourth week we try for a run-through of the entire program from the first curtain to the last bow. This is sometimes called a stagger-through. Many notes

Canadian choreographer Fernand Nault enjoyed great success for many years with his version of *Carmina Burana*, which integrates large forces of orchestra, solo and chorus singers, and dancers. Shown here in our 1997 production is Éric Beauchesne as the roasted swan, testament to a young dancer's muscularity. Also from the tavern scene in the same ballet is Malcolm Low.

are taken, both for the dancers and for us, the staff. The last ten percent is the hardest, we tell the dancers, and if the devil is in the details, it's the details that are the devil. We still feign calm and add more meetings to each crowded day.

"Well, isn't that a surprise! Bobby looks great!"

"Melissa is glowing. Is there something we don't know?"

"Philip is holding together very well, he's a powerhouse that boy. He's ready for a job, isn't he? Only fifteen? Has he finished school yet?"

"Patty's feet would definitely look better with another make of shoes. Suzie can you look into that?"

"David, you've done wonders with Roger, not only in class but also in the gym. He's much stronger! Bravo!"

"I swear Polly's put on at least a few ounces, thank heaven."

Sunday of this week is usually a picnic day. We travel out to a small lake at the base of Cascade Mountain, called Cascade run-off, issue dire warnings about too much mountain sun, and watch the young gods at play in a truly glorious setting. The tiny bathing

Young Heather Ogden first studied with Annette Jakabowsky in
Vancouver. Her first Odette, in the 1998 Training Course performances,
was coached by another Swan Queen, Annette av Paul. Heather went
on to become a principal dancer with the National Ballet of Canada

suits seem tinier. The more daring of the group plunge into the cold mountain water. Occasional tourists gawk at such extraordinary energy and fitness. A football appears. The boys seem suddenly tireless. Hamburgers and hot dogs are grilled. Two weeks from now there will be tears and goodbyes, but not just yet.

## WEEK FIVE

The run-throughs have not yet shown what the dancers are going to produce for the public. This is the week we start to make the age-old and always difficult transfer from studio to stage and so we move into another mode. The first time in the theatre we devote a special half-hour to an orientation session for those dancers unfamiliar with stage drills and precautions. By now the electrics and technical crew are hard at it; lights have been hung and focused very precisely. A linoleum covering is taped to the stage floor. Our lighting expert, Harry Frehner, starts his magic, often astonishing the dancers with changes of space and colour, moving the performance we have prepared into new proportions and textures; his little stick figures have led to LX cues that will eventually become computer-driven. Our co-ordinator collects program notes; sometimes a title will be changed at the last minute. Costumes are complete, now needing only the tiniest adjustments. If the alternate cast needs more time on stage, it will happen.

For the first few days spacing the dances is everything. Spacing and unison. If corps work is ragged when togetherness is essential it can spell a major problem; in certain choreographies heads, arms, footwork, body angles, and musicality have to become a canvas that effortlessly beguiles the eye. Unison. Musicians are used to this requirement, but then they have a conductor guiding them. Dancers have no such help. Rehearsal and schooling are their only way of achieving the alchemy of moving as one body. When unison is required, it should be thrilling, whether in a classical ballet or a cancan. If you haven't achieved it in the studio it will be immediately apparent on stage, unwittingly drawing attention to itself.

In week five a *répétiteur* will suddenly see, onstage, a detail that was not visible in the studio, so corrections and reminders for the dancers intensify. This can be trying. Patience is much needed and the young dancer must simply accept this as yet another attribute of professionalism. Suddenly, there seems to be very little time left. After technical rehearsals (with lights and props as needed) will come dress rehearsals, when we should finally glimpse the full effect of everyone's dedication. Sometimes this totality is lost on the busy young dancer.

"These tights are too big."

"Mine are too small. Should we trade?"

"Are the lights going to be that bright?"

"I'll never get that wretched pirouette. Help!"

"Do I need to shave for the photo call?"

"There are still pins in my jacket!"

"What do you mean it's different? I've always done it that way."

"I think my back's going into spasm!"

"O God, I've just blanked. What comes next?"

"Who moved my towel?"

"Sit down, relax for a minute, while I give some notes ..." The rapt attention and focus of these dancers during the 2001 program is probably repeated hundreds of times every day, all over the world. They are young, hopeful, motivated, and at their age, indestructibly determined.

Tara Birtwhistle, principal dancer, and Sasha Gamayunov, soloist, both with the Royal Winnipeg Ballet, are seen against forest, the immutable Cascade Mountain, and the ever-shifting clouds that remind us at Banff of the ephemeral nature of dance and dancing, and our brief involvement in an eternal practice.

What do these seven dancers have in common, apart from all being in the Professional Program in 2004, and probably being somewhat out of breath from having climbed to a perch by Cascade Falls? *From left to right:* Robert Pleshke is now with the Royal Winnipeg Ballet, Tiffany Bilodeau is a very strong member of Ballet Kelowna, Grace Hamley is dancing in the Netherlands, Reveriano Camil has returned to Mexico, Craig Samok has retired, and Leigh Allardyce and Kelley McKinlay are a couple, and dancing with the Alberta Ballet. The girls, as you can see, work at staying skinny and strong. The boys get strong lifting the skinny girls and making them appear weightless. They all share considerable stamina, the flame of dance, and not an ounce of fat among them.

"I think there's a positive energy, even from the mountains!" — J.M.

Attending a 1999 performance of the Professional Program, and seen in the foyer of the Eric Harvie Theatre
is a group of major players in the Canadian dance world.

*On the floor*: John Alleyne, choreographer and Artistic Director of Ballet British Columbia

*Seated*: Jeanne Renaud, choreographic pioneer, former Artistic Director of Les Grands Ballets
    Canadiens, and founder of Le Groupe de la Place Royale

André Lewis, Artistic Director of the Royal Winnipeg Ballet

Arnold Spohr, Artistic Director Emeritus of the Royal Winnipeg Ballet, Associate Artistic Director
    of Ballet Jörgen

Annette av Paul, founding director of Ballet British Columbia and Associate Program Director of
    the Dance Program at The Banff Centre

Standing: Valerie Wilder, now Executive Director of the Boston Ballet

Shawn Hounsell, 1997 Clifford E. Lee Choreographic Award recipient

Mikko Nissenen, now Director of the Boston Ballet

Standing, back row: Brian Macdonald, choreographer

Allen Kaeja, 1999 Clifford E. Lee Choreography Award recipient and Co-Artistic Director
    of Kaeja d'Dance.

"Is it all right if I dye my hair?"

"I feel sick!"

"I can't believe I messed up my solo like that."

WEEK SIX

The dress rehearsals have a relentless quality. Photographers hover and there are quick photo calls. Out there onstage, in the lights, lurk demons, pitfalls, and insecurities. The dancers are, after all, young and vulnerable. Expectations are high. We are all here to dance *enfin*. For us, the staff, it is important to be encouraging, excited and conversely imperturbable, but above all, calm. There is always time for helpful corrections. We are still occupied with the Training Course but for the Professional Course we have done our utmost to prepare for these performances. No more nagging. We have taught, choreographed, cajoled, explained, suggested, pleaded, demanded, and mined the vein of tough love as deeply as possible. The two dress rehearsals have helped to pull a lot together and what was a disparate group of dancers six weeks ago is now a very presentable little company. The effect of this intense six weeks is to propel the young dancer toward clear decisions. After opening night there are career discussions with those who ask for them.

"I love it. I love it. … at least for now."

"I want this life. What should I do next?"

"Maybe it's not for me. I don't have that kind of dedication."

'I want to do more contemporary movement, that's for sure."

"My boyfriend wants to get married."

"Should I audition in Europe?"

"What are my chances in the dance world?"

"My father wants me to be a lawyer. What should I tell him?"

The public should not be asked to make allowances. The dancer must be totally committed. We say it again. "Enhance the night." "Support each other." "Do it!" "Concentrate." "Dance!"

Six weeks have flown by.

*Losing Ground*, choreography Sabrina Mathews

# Clifford E. Lee
# Choreography Adward

IN 2006, THE BANFF CENTRE adopted a new logo, characterizing in two words what happens here among the mountains, lakes, and forests. The logo not only encapsulates what happened in the past, what is happening now, and what will continue to happen, but also speaks of how we wish the world to perceive us. The two words "Inspiring Creativity" capture brilliantly everything The Banff Centre represents.

A major gift to ensure perennial creativity for the summer Dance Program has been the Clifford E. Lee Foundation's award for choreography. Clifford E. Lee was a canny, Alberta-born entrepreneur who began his career as a teacher and also obtained a degree in pharmacy. He soon became an active member of the Cooperative Commonwealth Federation (CCF), which later became the New Democratic Party. Still

later, he and a friend started NuWest Homes, and the endeavor rapidly expanded to become the largest builder of homes in Alberta. The result of this early investment and the success of his other company, Dispensaries Ltd., a pharmaceutical company, created a significant personal fortune for Lee. Following his retirement in 1969, he and his wife, Lila, created a foundation, endowing it with the majority of his shares in NuWest Development. The foundation allowed him to balance the discrepancy between his social and political values and his accumulated wealth. Though he had hoped to devote his later years to philanthropic works, he died soon after establishing the foundation. However, the Clifford E Lee Foundation's careful guidelines identified various charities and areas for continuing support, including First Nations' causes, health and environmental issues, social services, and the arts. The foundation provided an extraordinary beginning for a choreographic award of international importance.

The late Ken Madsen, a long-time director of The Banff Centre, is generally considered to have been the tenacious parent of the idea of a choreographic award, and the man who greatly influenced the Lee Foundation to nurture that *rara avis*, a choreographer.

The Clifford E. Lee Choreography Award was started in 1978 and generously maintained until 1999. At that time an added gift to the endowment guaranteed that the Lee Award for an emerging choreographer would be granted in perpetuity at The Banff Centre. The award has become a magnet for young Canadian choreographers anxious to plunge into the complexities of creating an original work. A cash award of $5000 is combined with a six-week residency at the Centre, thirty-five to forty young dancers from the professional course with whom to create, modest production values, and four public performances of the finished dance.

The Lee Award choreographers recipients are all very different. Some are inexperienced and start to create quite tentatively, others, especially those previously deprived of opportunities to work with large groups (say sixteen to twenty) are raring to go. The program may suddenly explode in a blizzard of new movement, all the dancers working in couples, everyone learning everything. Or he or she may shun the pressure of a big group waiting to be activated and prefer to have only one or two couples, or just the men to start with. The staff tries hard to oblige, whatever the request.

I've found that asking choreographers to verbalize about their not-yet-born creation is always a trap. It's about "losing ground" or "light failing" or "lost gods" or "excavating ascent" or "I don't know yet." All I hope for and say clearly is, "create a new piece, full of dancing, okay? That's what we're here for."

The creations are nearly always loaded with invention and are exciting for everyone concerned, even if the thrust is not always clear. No matter. Let the dancers bring what they will to the choreography. See where it goes. This is the place and time to experiment, explore, take a new path, climb every ... Well, that's obvious, isn't it? Just go for it.

When Edward Hillyer was the Lee Award recipient in 1991 a very considerable choreographic talent was revealed, one that merited strong encouragement. The Award represents for a young artist a very big step. Once given, subsequent opportunities can be hard to come by. The larger dance companies often hesitate to allot finances and/or time to a relative newcomer. Choreographic workshops nearly always are pressure cookers, revealing little. It is often a smaller company that can provide that next chance to create. Advice to a young choreographer? Look to the smaller company. Don't wait.

The young American Mark Godden, when he arrived to the RWB, had switched from acting to dancing only in his early twenties studying both classical and contemporary movement. In 1989 when he arrived in Banff to choreograph his Lee Award piece we, the staff, were astonished by his preparedness. He knew his music intimately and had very strong ideas for the décor (columns of neon light against a black backdrop). He made a choice of dancers quickly but carefully, and started to work the afternoon of the first day. His ideas and movement were fresh and innovative from the very first rehearsal. He asked for an almost animalistic speed, what I call an "American" speed, and mirrored the propulsive score by Joan Tower with total confidence. *Sequoia* was a very successful ballet and later entered the repertoire of the RWB.

The choreographer is selected by a jury made up of major figures in the Canadian dance world. After studying the submitted videos, the jury whittles down the choice of applicants to two or three, and then wrangles over the final decision with the grave understanding that a new talent will benefit and grow considerably from this opportunity. The nominee is asked to consider using Canadian music, and to double-cast so that as many dancers as possible are included in the creative process.

To date some twenty-eight choreographers have seen their work come to life on the stage of the Eric Harvie Theatre. Vulnerable, every one of them, and promising, although perhaps not very experienced, they have been supported by the Lee Foundation's help and by the creative objective at the core of The Banff Centre. Each choreographer has taken the opportunity very seriously, but they have, naturally, varied enormously in talent and approach.

One man, who worked in contemporary movement, at the last minute wanted the dancers drenched in water. We managed to persuade him that not only was this a decision in which the dancers should have some choice, but that the soaked floor just might be slightly hazardous, MGM and Gene Kelly notwithstanding.

One young lady, now enjoying a very successful career, created her first major ballet in neo-classical movement with the somewhat medieval ambiance of chivalry. The ballet was full of sly humour, and when it was performed for an audience, provoked much laughter. "But it wasn't supposed to be that funny," the choreographer kept saying, "it's not my fault!"

Crystal Pite's *Quest* is as much about the futilities of battle and war as it is about the absurdities of chivalry. The context is medieval, the message is for today. Laughter greases the message.

*L'Etiquette*. Choreographed to movements by Bach, Corelli, and Vivaldi by Joe Laughlin, this was nothing if not subversive. It was as multi-layered in intent as in costuming, the men in cream-coloured full-sleeved shirts and gartered tights seeming bored, aristocratic, and dangerous; the women painted and bustiered, only slightly less mannered, all presided over by a faux marquise who might just have been a man. Everyone was dressed but seemed to be half-dressed or undressed. It wasn't set in a bordello exactly, but there was an undercurrent of nonchalant depravity disguised in period dances and gestures, rouged demeanours, gold shoes, and deadpan seductions. It was cruelly funny, original, and a brilliant success, later danced by the Royal Winnipeg Ballet.

"I was six years in the Dance Program.
When I got my job I was already
experienced and motivated." — K.M.

Another year, a talented newcomer cried a lot in frustration while she created, there being obviously some internal ferment plaguing her. Though what exactly none of us could figure out, even after she put her female dancers in short black tutus and army boots! Interesting movement, cathartic costuming. Why not?

An immensely clever young man created lovely movement but felt impelled to add twenty television monitors crowded with images to the stage, plus an emcee who was sometimes in a business suit and other times naked and talked in strangled animal sounds. Maybe he was rebelling against a brave new world; it never became quite clear.

Another choreographer unexpectedly costumed everyone in bright, orange tights, tops, leotards, and shoes — a Minute Maid commercial that did not go well with the Schoenberg Chamber Symphony. He had choreographed a good dance that came alive only when he was persuaded to let the dancers wear their varied street clothes. No orange.

One year, the dancers were obliged to climb in and out of green garbage bags to a Stravinsky score. This included some writhing and rolling about, clear and inexpensive symbolism.

In *Excavating Ascent*, there was a unisex feeling, with men and women used in a multiplicity of ways. The dancers were dressed in similar briefs, with kneepads evident. Choreographer Allen Kaeja came from the wrestling side of sport, and this was incorporated into the sculptural quality of the groupings, and his work's dominant sense of athleticism. Metal benches caught the light almost more than the dancers, imparting a sense of muscularity versus space and metal. The space was constantly shifting, with smoke alternately hiding and revealing the dancers. There was conflict and hard-edged rigour in the movement. The music seemed layered on top of the choreography, not inherent to it, but altogether the work was very challenging for the dancers.

Over the years it became apparent that the Clifford E. Lee Choreography Award was certainly encouraging creativity in the Dance Department. Although choreographers' works sometimes revealed a lack of skill in using large groups, and at other times evidenced a curious lack of stagecraft, a great deal of inventive and imaginative movement flowed on many occasions. Being able to think organically while deciding on scenic elements, envisioning careful and expressive lighting, and conceiving simple and original costuming all signify hard-to-come-by practical choreographic experience. But several ballets created with the Foundation's assistance were taken into other repertoires, and the Lee Award continues to help all along the way, truly inspiring creativity.

Wen Wei Wang came from China to Vancouver and from there to Banff. When he won the Lee Award in 2000, he brought with him several sensibilities that included a classical background and a talent to absorb and invent new movement that became quite wonderful choreography. He called his creation *Snow*, and that is what fell on the dancers at the final curtain. He has since embarked on a career as a solo performer, and is still finding new movement, very far from the strictures of his classical training. He is seen here with the still-growing Kelley McKinlay.

## Past recipients of the Clifford E. Lee Choreography Award

| | | |
|---|---|---|
| 1978 | Mauryne Allan | *Spring* |
| 1979 | Judith Marcuse | *Sadhana Dhoti* |
| 1980 | Renald Rabu | *Sparks* |
| 1981 | Jennifer Mascall | *Acoustic Noose* |
| 1982 | Stephanie Ballard | *Light Failing* |
| 1983 | Martine Époque | *Constellation 1* |
| 1984 | NOT AWARDED | |
| 1985 | Constantin Patsalas | *Notturni* |
| 1986 | Christopher House | *Go Yet Turning Stay* |
| 1987 | David Earle | *Cloud Garden* |
| 1988 | Randy Glynn | *Capricciosa* |
| 1989 | Mark Godden | *Sequoia* |
| 1990 | Howard Richard | *... And There You Are, All Alone Togerher* |
| 1991 | Edward Hillyer | *De Profundis* |
| 1992 | Lola MacLaughlin | *Waterwheel* |
| 1993 | Bengt Jörgen | *Bonds of Affection* |
| 1994 | Michael Downing | *Channel* |
| 1995 | Crystal Pite | *Quest** |
| 1996 | Gioconda Barbuto | *Chiaroscuro* |
| | Joe Laughlin | *L'Etiquette** |
| 1997 | Shawn Hounsell | *Creaturehood** |
| 1998 | Gaétan Gingras | *Shaping Worlds as Fire Burns* |
| 1999 | Allen Kaeja | *Excavating Ascent* |
| 2000 | Wen Wei Wang | *Snow* |
| 2001 | NOT AWARDED | |
| 2002 | Benjamin Hatcher | *Covenant* |
| 2003 | Andrew Giday | *Maelstrom* |
| 2004 | D.A. Hoskins | *Configurations of the Body* |
| 2005 | Sabrina Matthews | *losing ground* |
| | Peter Quanz | *Quantz by Quanz* |
| 2006 | Simone Orlando | *Winter Journey* |

* Also presented during the 2000 all Lee Award program.

*Configurations of the Body.* When D.A. Hoskins won the Lee Award in 2004, he came with a very strong recommendation from a fellow faculty member at Ryerson University. We knew very little about him. Would he use the award well? Truthfully, we did not know what to expect. He choreographed a very beautiful, mature, and inventive piece, flowing, mysterious, and clearly original. His work was somehow both geometric and erotic; barely clothed dancers, in white costumes, moved ceremoniously on a black floor taped out in quadrants. The movement was intricate and structured to include a lot of partnering, challenging the dancers, but not outdistancing them. Near the end of the work the dancers carried white boxes of various heights onto the stage and simply stood on them; a kind of living museum of sculptured figures.

*Losing Ground*

"The intensity sure marks you.  It tells you
what it takes to have a career." — X.X.

"Banff has a reputation for slingshooting a dancer
into a career. That's what it did for me!" — C.G.

Seen here in 1978 in the skating pas de deux from *Tam ti Delam*,
Annette av Paul and David LaHay are now co-directors of the Summer
Dance Program and the Banff Festival Ballet. This duet is tricky and
lighthearted. Conquering it together cemented a lifelong friendship.

# 1982

IN 1982, AS PART OF the plan to enhance the Dance Program, I decided to continue the policy of inviting guest teachers of international calibre each summer. Mrs. Farrally was initially worried that if any of the senior dancers, after exposure to the highest standard of instruction and coaching, decided to move away from their home studios, we would be accused of all manner of unprofessionalism, or at least malfeasance, and jealousies would be unleashed. Studios in the dance world can be prone to husbanding and guarding their best talents. I assured her that if it had not happened in the past it would not suddenly occur in the future. So a number of top teachers, although not necessarily of RAD lineage, continued to be invited to teach our newly designated

Professional Course. Olga Lepeshinskaya (Bolshoi Ballet), Maria Fay (Royal Ballet), Laura Alonso (Cuban Ballet), Olga Evreinoff (Kirov Ballet), Michael Byars, Victoria Simon, Pat Neary and Violette Verdy (New York City Ballet), and Raymond Smith (National Ballet of Canada) were among them. Auditions across Canada became more rigorous, audition videotapes were invited from "foreign" (mostly US) students, and our reputation as a demanding program, far from the slur of "summer camp," could only grow.

The Professional Program grew in length from five to six weeks. Everything was put in place to provide technical support for the presentation of challenging choreography of an international calibre. It was all part of the plan for enhancement. My own career furnished contacts upon whom I was quick to call. Balanchine, Ashton, Cranko, the emerging Kenneth MacMillan, and even Celia Franca would be encouraged to become, however briefly each summer, part of our total picture.

By 1982, my work *Aimez-vous Bach?* had been taken up by six or eight international companies and I had become adept at teaching the work as concisely as possible. The ballet started its life at Banff as a series of contrapuntal exercises (I thought then that *Pointe Counterpointe* was a really snappy title) and had become quite a popular calling card for me. *Aimez-vous Bach?* had not only won an award at a Paris festival but had also become a staple in many companies. It seemed fitting to present the ballet again in Banff in the first year of enrichment of the Professional Program.

The mandate for expansion also aimed to abet the development of the Alberta Ballet, particularly in the way of summer work and performances. Their fourteen dancers joined fourteen of our young professionals to make a company of twenty-eight, a fine size for this ballet that had been danced by casts varying in number from sixteen to thirty-six. For the dancers already a generation away from the original 1962 cast, the fit of jazz movement to the fugue accompanying the *D Minor Toccata* was a surprise and only a little shocking. Boris Brott conducted the Calgary Philharmonic, so some very well-played Bach spurred the dancers on. *Aimez-vous Bach?* opened the program.

Danced by a sparkling, technically strong couple, the pas de deux from *Don Quixote* (*Don Quichotte* in French, or "*Don Q.*" in dancers' slang) is frequently disparaged by being referred to as an "old war-horse".

Researching the meaning of "war-horse" provided few clues for such an epithet being attached to the pas de deux.

"The term originated in the mid 1600s for a military charger that had been through many battles. In the 1800s it began to be used for human veterans, and in the mid 1900s for popular productions, especially of musical works."

(*The American Heritage Dictionary of Idioms*).

Does that make *Eine Kleine Nachtmusik*, Ravel's *Bolero*, Tchaikovsky's *Swan Lake* or *Smoke Gets in Your Eyes* eligible for the same epithet? Maybe *Clair de Lune*, *The Moonlight Sonata*, any Hungarian Rhapsody, Rachmaninoff's *C# Minor Prelude*, or even *Chopsticks* belong too. Surely *Celeste, Aida*, *La Donna e Mobile*, *Visse d'Arte*, and *Begin the Beguine* would qualify along with *Variations on a Theme* by Paganini, Beethoven's Fifth, *Don't Fence Me In* and *The Warsaw Concerto*. Why leave out the danced *Don Q.*?

The full-length ballet from which the pas de deux is derived is almost never performed today. The music by Leon Minkus is straightforward music hall, the costumes are too often the black and orange of Halloween baubles, and the choreography has been considerably tinkered with since its birth on December 26th, 1869.

*Aimez-vous Bach?*

"Banff was the RWB
school before we
had a school!"
— A.S.

This was my favourite studio when I began teaching jazz, pas de deux and the men's class in the early 1960s. The room was called The Solarium because it was windowed on three sides. Forests, mountains, and sunlight, coupled with a clear view down the Bow Valley, made dancing easier, we all felt, even the floor exercises. The space was also used for conferences and as a lounge, and at one point, some years later, housed a smoky bar. Gweneth would sometimes watch my class here as I taught, among others, Jennifer Penney, Donna Day Washington, Virginia Wakelyn, Richard Cragun, and Reid Anderson, with the valley winds and racing clouds our only audience.

Still, *Don Q.* is a very sturdy piece, showy, brilliant, and popular; not quite the trappings of an old war-horse. True, the dancers who can master it usually assume a hauteur and pseudo-Spanish demeanour that includes proud nostrils, tossings of the head, and the odd snort. At a Moscow competition, I once saw one of the competitors, a young, unknown Argentinian dancer, just a few seconds into the entree of *Don Q.*, throw himself into such a high and perfect leap, with stallion-like power, that the judges and public gasped, knowing that in that instant, a gold medallist had been born. His tiny partner likewise astonished the crowd with a series of *pas de cheval* (little pawing steps) executed on pointe, rapid, clean, and coltish.

In short, if dancers can master this duet, making light of all its tricks and proud posturing, it becomes a brilliant showpiece, high-spirited and highly entertaining. Let's never call it an old war-horse. It is for the young to hurdle, entering the winner's circle before they get too old.

In our 1982 program, Laura Alonso, of the famous Cuban Alonsos, taught and coached *Don Quixote* for two different couples. She passed on not only steps, but also traditions to dancers Svea Eklof, Alejandro Menéndez, Marianne Beausejour and Scott Harris, who performed the duet with happy, unbridled abandon.

The Lee Award creation for 1982 was Stephanie Ballard's *Light Failing*. Her program note read: "Often when people meet on mutual ground, natural patterns evolve and ritual is established. Sometimes it's best to simply let things be and accept light failing."

However, despite her ambitious choreographic intentions, Stephanie's ballet did not have a strong impact. But to quote from her own recollections, "Now with some perspective, I can look at my work and the entire experience with considerable clarity. Banff was indeed a turning point for me both personally and professionally. It was essential to my artistic growth and had a tremendous effect on shaping my dance career. My abilities as a choreographer grew enormously. Even though *Light Failing* did not work as it could have, the process did work as it should have."

I had seen John Cranko's comic success *Pineapple Poll* in the repertoire of the Sadler's Wells Theatre Ballet when it came to Toronto in the early 1950s. Some thirty years later I felt it would be a wonderful challenge within the new direction of the Banff program. Cranko, who had become a friend, stayed with me in Tel Aviv while creating a new work for the Batsheva company in the early 1960s. He was a very likeable and good-humoured man, bubbling with ideas for new work, witty stories, and no small measure of mischief. His experience in revue and cabaret had sharpened his love of drolleries of a very British kind. In fact, his first choreographic success was based on *The Bumboat Woman's Story* from W. S. Gilbert's *Bab Ballads*. A frothy tale of the topsy-turvydom that characterized the famous W. S., it had been set to a score purloined from Sir Arthur Sullivan's bag of popular tunes that made up his very successful operettas: *Trial by Jury, The Mikado, Patience, Ruddigore, Princess Ida, The Gondoliers, The Pirates of Penzance*, and others — accessible music of a distinctively popular sparkle. Cranko had happened on a truly funny situation, a comic invention, set in Portsmouth harbour.

The plot of *Pineapple Poll* involves sailors (their ship is called the *Hot Cross Bun*), their sweethearts, Jaspar, a potboy from a nearby tavern, Poll, a very attractive street seller, the handsome and highly desirable Captain Belaye whose every glance or even jig-step makes girls swoon with love sickness, Blanche, his fiancée, and her chaperone-aunt, Mrs. Dimple. The girls disguise themselves as bearded sailors to gain access to the ship, but they take to the Captain's drill very badly and when his cannon goes off, Poll faints. All is discovered and wrongs righted in the final melee. The Captain, married to Blanche, becomes an admiral; Jaspar, incredibly, becomes a captain and thus beloved by Poll; the sailors are reconciled with their girlfriends; and even Mrs. Dimple becomes Britannia incarnate. Need I add that disbelief becomes more than suspended? It is, by the merry finale, badly damaged amid the fun.

Reid Anderson, who had been in my boys' classes in Banff for several years, had since become a principal dancer with John Cranko's company in Stuttgart. Along with his companion Dieter Graf, the heir to Cranko's estate, he arranged for us to mount *Pineapple*

*Poll* that summer of 1982 and came to teach it. We copied the original designs by Osbert Lancaster and had a whale(!) of a time. The complete production was subsequently given to the Alberta Ballet.

While the critical establishment is inclined to belittle this gem of a ballet, it is ingeniously constructed, as swiftly told as a good joke, and a minor masterpiece of invention. Even high in the mountains of Banff, well away from Portsmouth and the shenanigans on the *Hot Cross Bun*, it was funny and seaworthy.

The great ladies of the Canadian dance scene were all invited to the opening of the newly invigorated Dance Program in Banff. When it was all over Gweneth Lloyd smiled benignly. Ludmilla Chiriaeff was very encouraging and felt that we had taken an excellent step to help young dancers develop. Celia Franca hated everything and was quite cruel in her criticisms.

*Light Failing*, Stephanie Ballard

In 1982, we presented *Pineapple Poll*. Above are Captain Balaye and the bearded ladies pretending to be sailors aboard the good ship *Hot Cross Bun*. Poll was an early and very successful comic ballet by choreographer John Cranko. This production was later danced by the Alberta Ballet Company.

*Big Band*: Recordings of Stan Kenton's orchestra, with its full-blooded sound and masterful arrangements, were part of the 1950s and 1960s (or could it have been the 1940s and 1950s?) for me. I had done several works for Les Ballets Jazz soon after that company was born. At Gweneth Lloyd's request, and with Eva von Gencsy as my assistant, I had taught jazz classes — this "new" movement and technique — in Banff since 1960. One of the works from the repertoire of Les Ballets Jazz, aptly called *Big Band*, seemed like a natural for the professional course in 1995. We jived, swung, jitterbugged, pirouetted on our knees, wore bobbysocks, and mellowed out, and a whole era came alive again. The 1995 dancers were too young to have known this rapture, but loved the reckless, off-balance, into-the-floor, "dig it, baby, dig it" steps of the period, the flamboyant physicality and sheer fun of slides and throws and "Latin hips," of actually dancing together, the boy and girl sexiness of the big band, with the screaming brass bringing joy to a new world of youth unlimited. What a treat! Forget your troubles, come on, get happy. Post-Charleston and pre-bop meant dancing to the big bands.

Annette av Paul, seen here in the first incarnation of *Time Out
of Mind* in Banff 1980 with her partner Dwight Shelton, brought
Swedish glamour (one journalist called her a "blonde tigress")
to a decor by the famed Czech designer Josef Svoboda. Annette
and Dwight subsequently danced *Time Out of Mind* all over the
world with Les Grands Ballets Canadiens.

# 1987

EARLY IN THE PROCESS OF assembling of this book, I determined that chronicling the activities and achievements of 1987 would offer a clear indication of the ambition and seriousness of the Professional Program. The works undertaken for performance that year included two masterpieces from the 1930s by George Balanchine and Léonide Massine, and two creations by Canadians David Earle and me. Mr. B.'s *Serenade*, known worldwide, was a challenge for a new company of youngsters. My *Breaks* combined a duo by Mozart with interpolations by Harry Freedman, commissioned by The Banff Centre for the occasion. David Earle's *Cloud Garden* was the Lee Award premiere, and *Gaîté Parisienne* was a co-production with the Royal Winnipeg Ballet, the revival of a near-forgotten, once-popular frivolity. It was a summer rich in accomplishment.

*Serenade*, then forty-three years old, was the first ballet Mr. B. created in the United States. It had quickly become a touchstone for the New York City Ballet. I had seen it many times in the early years of the NYCB, and in fact I have kept programs on which I carefully noted certain steps and groupings that were particularly felicitous. I had rehearsed the ballet when I was in Stockholm with the Royal Swedish Ballet, and later brought it into the repertoire of Les Grands Ballets Canadiens. We had done *Four Temperaments* in 1986, and I was delighted when it became possible for us to stage *Serenade* in Banff.

The ballet is a cascade of invention and beauty. Much has been written about it by dance scholars and many interpretations of its meaning advanced, but it guards its secrets well. There are descriptions of how, in early rehearsals one girl fell and another arrived late, and stories of how these and other studio incidents were incorporated, supposedly as part of classes on stage technique, into a work that metamorphosed into an extraordinary and hauntingly timeless ballet.

I must add that I don't believe many of the conjectures as to the story, or implications of hidden meanings in the choreography, or even what has been written by Balanchine himself. But I have for many years been troubled by certain questions:

If *Serenade* is a study in stagecraft, why did Balanchine choose that music? Tchaikovsky's elegant mixture of melancholy and energy are at odds with the avowed objective. Why not Haydn or Czerny? Why did Mr. B. reverse the third and fourth movements? For reasons

"I was given the first scholarship as a jazz dancer. It changed my life." — J.P.

The young and very straight-backed Tara Birtwhistle from the Royal Winnipeg Ballet in mid-air, and Michael Doerner from the National Ballet in a 1993 Banff production of *Time Out of Mind*. How does she land from that position? That's our secret.

of theatricality alone? But why? Why did he choose some of the steps and nearly all the gestures? The final exit, with a dancer being held aloft as though to embrace a far-off, brilliant light — again, why?

Sometimes I reason that if a choreographer started out to argue for the holding back of death a little longer, to dance to the edge of time before finally accepting the inevitability of mortality, he might very well have chosen this music and fashioned this choreography and, in the name of an exercise in stagecraft, disguised his deepest preoccupations, particularly if he were Russian.

*Pace*, Balanchine, who said, "Many people think there is a concealed story in the ballet. There is not. There are, simply, dancers in motion to a beautiful piece of music. The only story is the music's story, a serenade, a dance, if you like, in the light of the moon."

Somewhere in this world *Serenade* will be danced tonight, somewhere it was danced last night, and somewhere it will be danced tomorrow night. As I write this in 2006 it is being taught and prepared again here in Banff, where we have already mounted it four times (1987, 1990, 1997, 2001).

*Breaks*, a commission by The Banff Centre, allowed me indulge myself with one of my favourite techniques, that of combining music from different decades or even different centuries to benefit from what is revealed; for instance, juxtaposing the symmetry of

"Even the RWB doesn't do that
much work in a day!" — C.L.

Baroque composition with the fragmentations and dichotomies of twentieth-century dis-
coveries. Harry Freedman wrote interpolations into the *Mozart Duo #2 for Violin and
Viola* for me. Spiked into the effortless-sounding Mozart melodies and harmonies were
more angst-driven serial textures of contemporary creativity. Freedman's interventions
yielded a remarkably cohesive score. For the dancers, it was music not only to dance *to*
but to dance *in*, deriving the impetus from within the sounds and structures, on a deeper
level than simply dancing to the music. This, of course, meant that I had to find choreography that became an amalgam of time and space and sound and that reached the public
on that special level that derived totally from what we were hearing and in the space given
us. It is a heady process, requiring dancers happy to join in the journey.

Most of the women were rehearsing *Serenade*, which needs nineteen female dancers,
every morning and a good part of the afternoon. I had to work around that schedule,
choosing four female soloists and eight eager men, dividing them into trios, at least for

*Breaks*, in 1987, with music by Mozart
and Freedman. Two different trios.

*Breaks*, with the quartet of two violins and two violas, to which the dancers continually play homage. The score, alternating between the music of two composers separated by more than two centuries, allows for a wide range of movement by the twelve dancers.

the first movement, stealing time from the other choreographers, and imperturbably going where inspiration led me.

Being artistic director of a program also means being a host. Being the boss allows no licence. I had Victoria Simon teaching *Serenade*, David Earle creating *Cloud Garden*, and Lorca Massine and Susanna della Pietra mounting *Gaité*. Meanwhile, I worked secretly on my *Breaks*. The breaks, of course, are with tradition. I finally added this information to the program note, which previously hadn't really explained much! I wanted to create a joyous piece. The Mozart literally danced off the page and into the studio space, only bringing the more serial Freedman into play to illustrate my thesis that sound is profound, always has been and always will be, and today's new sounds perpetuate a need to reveal beauties unspoken unless we search for them.

The second movement of the Mozart, the adagio, was prefaced by Freedman's "take" on it. With an introduction in serial vocabulary, it became three pas de deux where the invention held fast and actually, as I had hoped for, was singularly at one with the music.

Beethoven's *Diabelli Variations* was a challenging experience for a Canadian naïf choreographing on the very fine dancers of the Paris Opera Ballet. I found that atmosphere exceedingly unsettling, with intrigues, strikes, jealousies, and drama in abundance. Somehow I survived, but only after deciding that while I would get my ballet finished and before the public on the vast and famous stage of the Palais Garnier, I would choreograph it again on another company when there were fewer fractious distractions. With Les Grands Ballets Canadiens, I edited the choreography, and was helped by Robert Prévost's excellent costumes and decor, befitting Montreal's Place des Arts. There was a magical improvement. Later at Banff, on the stage of the Eric Harvie Theatre, and with more editing (!), the ballet came wonderfully alive. *Enfin*. Viva Banff!

In *Findings* (1983), I grappled with aspects of society that defy nouns, verbs, or even psychological theories, using dancers to fashion new or often hidden messages. That sounds pretentious I'm sure, but choreographers have ways of unearthing meanings, otherwise unfound except perhaps by poets. Bodies have many languages, sometimes imprecise or half-formed, sometimes stunningly unique to the human condition, so we must search.

The moon-like grid was the work of sculptor Claude Girard. The music was Bach, interspersed by two paraphrases of the theme from *Musical Offering* by Serge Garant. I remember being challenged by a six-voice fugue and being rewarded by achieving the complexity it demanded.

The third movement wove Mozart and Freedman into a little tapestry of contrasts that Harry sewed together with a genial touch. I was very happy choreographing this piece, especially for a program that included Tchaikovsky, Offenbach, and a range of traditional Japanese music. *Breaks* is only about music and dance. The musicians are on a platform far upstage, eight or ten feet off the ground, framed by black drapes. The dancers first listen, then dance. The music is like a mist in the air above them.

*Cloud Garden* proved to be quite demanding, rather like its choreographer, David Earle. Eventually he came up with a scenario and set to work.

"The old poet hides from Death, but Death is everywhere. He is caught but escapes to see another year. Three stories are told to pass the time in the journey from Spring Blossoms to bare-branched Winter. As the year passes, the poet has an opportunity to choose the moment of his death, and make it a gift."

The dancers responded well to David Earle's vocabulary. With a few rocks in the background, white, spare costumes, and a compelling sense of ceremony, he contrived a very moving piece, full of insights into stoicism and ceremony. I think he grew to respect the contribution the dancers were making to his stark tale, and to forgive their lack of "contemporary" training and make the most of the skills they brought. He insisted on bringing in a guest, the superb Learie McNicolls, for the Death figure, and danced

"The bed is like a wafer of sunlight." The poet's image is translated into sculpture, one part of the stage setting of *The Shining People of Leonard Cohen*. Seen here in a 1993 Banff production, Amanda Daft and Dominic De Wolfe portray the lovers. This ballet was originally commissioned by the Royal Winnipeg Ballet from choreographer Brian Macdonald, composer Harry Freedman, and sculptor Ted Bieler.

*Lost Gods*. Years later, I went back to the four protagonists of *Double Quartet*, realizing that they had a further destiny, and that the plague would rob them of their youngest member. Tara Birtwhistle, Paul Destrooper, Brandon Downs and David Lucas came from the Royal Winnipeg Ballet to become the clay for this sad epilogue. They inspired and helped four dancers from the Banff course who were the second cast, and went on to perform both Schafer's *String Quartet No.1* and *No.5* in a taping for Bravo! *Double Quartet* was coupled with *God's Children* to create the television production titled *Lost Gods*. Banff, R. Murray Schafer, and fine dancers were the catalysts.

In the aftermath of 9/11, I was one of millions gripped with grief. Soon, I was moved by the idea of choreographing the Verdi *Requiem*. I conceived of it not only as a requiem for lives shattered by hatred, but for all humanity's inhumanities, and for the murdering of peace that flows through the blood of history like an unforgiving and unstoppable poison.

I approached John Cripton, the impresario and producer, to forward the project. We both felt Banff was the place to start. We brought four dancers from the Royal Winnipeg Ballet, combining them with the professional course and John marshalled the forces — designer Astrid Janson, National Arts Centre Orchestra conductor Mario Bernardi, soloists, and choir, and secured two performances at the National Arts Centre.

More than half the *Requiem* was choreographed at Banff in the summer of 2002. Again, the Centre became the ideal situation to nurture and develop ideas, to let Verdi's music echo down the valley, and to balance grief and rage by affirming life through dance. We used projections of ruins and long-gone civilizations as our backdrop and let young dancers lament the past, the present, and the unknowable future.

This 1987 photo of the last pose of the cancan in *Gaîté Parisienne*, probably taken at a dress rehearsal, illustrates exactly what will happen next. Much remains to be "cleaned up" in a subsequent session with a ballet master or ballet mistress, bloodhounds with sharp eyes who gnaw at every detail until a performance is ready for the public. Corrections, corrections, corrections.

"Heads front on the last note, everyone please."

"Hands flexed, right arm higher than the left."

"Skirts held just under the chin so I can see those smiling faces."

"No flexed feet, ladies."

"If you're out of breath, don't let the audience hear you gasp. Boys especially!"

"Let Svea judge the applause ... when she starts to get up, we all move."

"And keep smiling. We're supposed to be having fun, probably after midnight in a Paris café. This cancan's not vulgar, even for a second. High spirits! High spirits!"

"We'll get to costume details later. Let's go from the top again, just for your stamina, and maestro, a touch faster this time please. Ladies, those kicks have to end up behind your ears. Boys, a little sizzle won't hurt ... watch your spacing on the second entrance. Here we go ... Oh, and do please try to dance together!"

Although the dancers were Canadian youngsters, far away from any major city — and especially far from the Parisienne demimonde, where Offenbach's sparkling melodies were the hits of the day — and few knew left bank from right, we had a world-famous ballet to dance, and had to sparkle our way through it in the most sophisticated way possible. This photo is good evidence of our trying. Claude Girard from Montreal designed the scenery and costumes. I especially loved the chandelier.

As I look at this photo, again and again I'm reminded that the brilliant young dancer in the centre, David Peregrine, died a year later when his private plane crashed into the Rockies.

the Old Poet himself, and even if the total echoed the Graham canon, the work made a fine contribution to the 1987 season. *Cloud Garden* was well received and was later added to the repertory of the Toronto Dance Theatre.

*Gaité Parisienne* was a brilliant and timely suggestion by Brydon Paige, associate director of the summer program and a close personal friend. Léonid Massine's light-hearted frolic, first mounted for the Ballet Russe de Monte Carlo in 1938, was for many years a deservedly popular hit. Set to various known and newly unearthed music by Offenbach, the ballet featured a collection of characters both enduring and witty who supposedly sprung from the *demimonde* of Paris, symbolizing the gaiety of la belle époque and particularly the Café Tortoni. The glove seller, the flower seller, the handsome baron, the ballet-master, cancan dancers, the elderly duke, the red lady (la lionne), waiters, soldiers, dandies, billiard players, maids, *cocodettes*, and a visiting rich eccentric Peruvian, were caught up in a whirl of flirtations and waltzes, mixing gaiety and sentiment in a *tourbillon* of tunes.

Nearly fifty years later this Paris *tarte à la crème* seemed to have vanished, but I had seen it in the repertoire of the Ballet Russe in the 1940s with the magical Danilova as the glove seller and Freddie Franklin as the dashing baron. I had a vivid memory, too, of a young Canadian named Pat Wilde, who later became a leading dancer for Mr. B. in the New York City Ballet, whipping off multiple *fouettés* with breathtaking élan while leading the cancan. I had also rehearsed the ballet in the 1960s when I was director of the Royal Swedish Ballet, although there it didn't have quite the same punch, the Swedes being of a rather solemn nature. It was there though, in the opera house in Stockholm, that I realized how cleverly eggs, sugar, and sentiment had been stirred together by Massine. *Gaité Parisienne* is the quintessential dessert for any meal.

Our manager in Banff, George Ross, found Lorca Massine, the choreographer's son and heir, and his assistant Susanna della Pietra, who could remember the ballet's every step and gesture. We persuaded the Royal Winnipeg Ballet to join us in a co-production. Four of their dancers came to Banff to learn and perform with the Professional Program, Svea Eklof and David Peregrine to learn the glove seller and the baron, John Kaminski the Peruvian, and Laura Graham to lead the cancan. Along with them came the RWB orchestra conductor Earl Stafford. Costumes and scenery were designed especially by Claude Girard from Montreal to reflect the epoch, as well as to survive the extensive touring and one-night stands that were the backbone of RWB's survival. The production, all the scenery, costumes, boots, props, feathers, gloves, gowns, hats, red drapes, and a gorgeous chandelier were made in Banff under Claude's supervision. We gave four performances and the dancers loved dancing *Gaité Parisienne*. Claude Caron as the Peruvian and Deborah Washington as the glove seller were to the manner born. On opening night, if not champagne, it was a fine sparkling wine, young perhaps, but with enough effervescence to evoke the original. Following the final performance, everything, even the orchestra parts, was bundled into a truck and whisked away to Winnipeg where the ballet was toured for several years. Eighteen months later there was a major revival by American Ballet Theatre and still later by the Paris Opera. I always felt that we in Banff could well have sparked those revivals...

*Canto Indio*, originally commissioned by Rebekah Harkness for New York City's Harkness Ballet, was premiered in Cannes in 1966 and danced worldwide by numerous companies. Here, Marianne Beausejour and Claude Caron of the Alberta Ballet dance in the Professional Program's 1985 production of the ballet. Carlos Chavez's music, *Sinfonia India*, is the inspiration for a flirtation between a bullfighter and a peasant girl, a showpiece for a talented couple.

The late John Stanzel taught and performed for a number of years in both the Summer Dance Program and the Musical Theatre Division. He is seen here in 1978 in one of his most famous roles, the vieux bonhomme in *Tam ti Delam*, with music by Gilles Vigneault and choreography by Brian Macdonald. Stanzel was the central figure who sang bits of doggerel, acted as the focal point, urging on the large company of dancers, and tapped and gigued throughout this enormously popular ballet.

A men's movement, often showy and fun, should allow them to shine. In *Tam ti Delam* they can bash at it a bit. It's in the genre and it should be lighthearted, infectious, and rousing. Should be? Must be!

*Tam ti Delam* is a ballet inspired by folk dance, originally created for Les Grands Ballets Canadiens, and set to a series of enormously popular songs by Quebecois composer and *chanteur* Gilles Vigneault. It has had over five hundred performances worldwide and is a hybrid of *danses carrés* and classical techniques with a glaze of showbiz. The fourth movement, a pas de deux that derives from skating moves, is a particular joy for both the public and the two dancers who master it. Here Nicole Caron, who spent several summers at Banff before joining the Alberta Ballet, is held aloft by Brad Brannan, now with the Royal Winnipeg Ballet.

In the finale of *Tam ti Delam*, there is a short recapitulation of the men's uptempo, show-off jumps and spins. Here Mark Patrocci illustrates just what a leap can be! Short of stature, virile of nature, and sturdy and smiling in stage presence, he is originally from New Brunswick, trained at the Royal Winnipeg Ballet School, and now dances in the United States. He speaks in an unexpectedly low register for his size, is unfailingly polite, and can jump like a jungle cat.

*Double Quartet* was originally created for Les Grands
Ballets Canadiens as a response to the R. Murray Schafer
*String Quartet No.1*, paired with Schubert's *Quartettsatz*.
The musicians of the Orford String Quartet shared the
stage with the dancers. What emerged was the bonding
and individuality of the players, reflected by the bonding
and interdependency of the dancers, driven by sometimes
joyous, sometimes dangerous movement.

# Balanchine at Banff

A YEAR BEFORE the official celebrations of the centenary of George Balanchine's birth, we all felt that we could challenge our young dancers, and also be first off the mark, by devising a program that covered the range of his extraordinary output. We therefore rehearsed and performed several ballets in their entirety: *Concerto Barocco*, *Donizetti Variations*, and *Who Cares?* We also selected certain movements of other ballets for performance: the first movement of *Serenade*, the second movement of *Symphony in C*, the men's movement of *Stars and Stripes*, and the final movement of *Theme and Variations*. To all this we added duets, the third Theme from *Four Temperaments*, the central duet from *Agon*, the complete Tchaikovsky *Pas de Deux*. We then mixed in various

*Serenade* was first performed in Banff in 1987, and is shown here in the 1997 performance. Barbara Moore, then a principal dancer with the Alberta Ballet Company, spent many summers in our professional program. Jean Grand-Maître trained at the École Supérieure in Montreal and is now Artistic Director of the Alberta Ballet Company and a choreographer with an international reputation. Tanya Evidente currently dances with the National Ballet of Canada.

trenchant observations by Mr. B. on choreography, music, and life, background anecdotes, projected film clips, and photos. We even had Violette Verdy fly into Banff to coach the Tchaikovsky *Pas de Deux*, which had been created on her when she was a principal dancer with the New York City Ballet. Her coaching was videotaped so that audiences could see her working with the very dancers who were about to dance on the Banff stage.

Overall, our celebration was an enormous undertaking. The Balanchine Trust *répétiteur*, Victoria Simon, taught everything, making extraordinarily efficient use of every hour of rehearsal, always emphasizing the qualities of the movement paramount to making the choreography fascinating to the audience. Costumes were made in our atelier, or borrowed from various sources. The Banff Centre's resident lighting designer, Harry Frehner, as skilled as any designer with whom I have ever worked, coordinated the lighting, projections, and live commentators. Somehow, miraculously, in five weeks and two days, we were ready!

Dancers from all across Canada — thus representing various teachers and diverse schoolings — were united by dancing choreographies all devised by the same Russian-American genius. Those fortunate dancers loved the experience. They were learning and rehearsing some of the finest choreography of the twentieth century. Certain of Mr. B.'s idiosyncrasies of technique were new to them. "It doesn't matter," was our message. "For this program, do what he had taught. Learn, and for the future, remember. That's why we're here."

Balanchine's musicality (Anna Kisselgoff of *The New York Times* once said "Mr. B. was the Bach of ballet") consisted not only of dancing on and in the beat, but also of asking yourself, why that step to that music? The lyricism of *Serenade* was obviously very different from the neo-classicism of Hindemith, or the singular, rich, contemporary signals of Stravinsky's *Agon*. "Be ready to respond," Balanchine implied, "and to be imbued with the music the way I am."

From a 1990 performance, this is the first image of *Serenade*, seen as the curtain rises, a moment at once mysterious, moonlit, and hushed. Nineteen young dancers in long dresses stand still, each with one arm and hand held up against the light ... Against time? Against death? There have been many interpretations of that first gesture. Suffice it to say that the moment is breathtaking, and so perfectly at one with Tchaikovsky's music that it stays with us long after the swirling, endless invention of Balanchine's choreography has finished.

Yseult Lendvai in the opening moment of *Serenade*, photographed in 1987. Trained at the École Supérieure in Montreal, and several times a participant in the Banff program, she danced professionally with Ballet British Columbia, the National Ballet of Canada and the Stuttgart Ballet, where she became a principal dancer under the direction of Reid Anderson (who was also a Banff participant). She has just recently retired.

*Agon* was a privilege for us to dance in 1994, forty years after
Mr. Balanchine created it for the New York City Ballet. Meaning
"contest," Agon is a plotless, abstract ballet characterized by
austere but extraordinary movement. The Stravinsky score moves
from a basically diatonic fanfare to strictly serial movements,
complex and at times overwhelmingly dense. There are twelve
dancers, four men and eight women.

   Although the ballet is supposedly based on seventeenth-
century French court dances, such connections seem tenuous.
*Agon* has an air of ritual and elusive fascination; it also appears
to be timeless, and not, as of this writing, fifty years old.

   Perhaps that is why its intellectual underpinnings can be
forbidding to our Banff audiences. *Agon* is a high mountain to
climb. Nothing, however, can diminish its greatness. Let me say
it again ... it is a privilege for us to dance *Agon*.

"Learn, and for the
future, remember.
That's why we're here."

We gave our first three performances in the small Margaret Greenham Theatre. This involved sacrificing onstage space with little room in the wings (although we had no scenery) but offered a tremendous gain in intimacy, allowing young dancers to gain the confidence to project in the bigger Eric Harvie Theatre to a bigger audience for a final gala. The program was all about dancing: dancing and music; old steps in new combinations, new steps to surprise and intrigue; steps devised to Bach, Hindemith, Tchaikovsky, and Gershwin; movement that demanded a faster way to move; formations that wove space and surprises; invention and wit.

Annette and David, Susie, guest teacher Margaret Mercier and Victoria Simon had all danced these ballets, some many times, but for the young dancers it was a very specific learning experience, provocative and infinitely rewarding. They grew before our eyes. Individually and together, different values surfaced in their dancing. They gained stamina and authority, became more grounded in technique, as well as faster, and braver, lingering in the air, and projecting Mr. Balanchine's intricate joy.

Balanchine's *Jewels*, which we mounted in Banff in 1995, displays three aspects of the maestro's musicality and techniques to music by Massenet, Stravinsky, and Tchaikovsky. These photos are of *Rubies*, the sharp-edged, inventive, and witty Stravinsky section.

Another of Balanchine's tapestries, *Divertimento No.15* is made for five
leading ballerinas and three principal men, plus a corps of eight women,
an unlikely combination that looks completely logical in the choreographic weaving. Solos, duets, trios, and groups flow seamlessly, with
unforced invention, in a manner as sunny and untroubled as Mozart's
music. The ballet is bewitching from start to finish, and when it is well

During the summer of our Balanchine tribute, performances included the second movement of *Symphony in C* (©The School of American Ballet). It starts simply, with the entrance of six corps girls. Feet, legs, and carriage are paramount. Elegance and youth count. Glamour helps.

Victoria Simon of the Balanchine Trust has taught Mr. B's technique and fourteen of his ballets, certain of them over several different years, to succeeding generations of dancers who may well make their first contact with the great choreographer's output at Banff. She is immensely knowledgeable, experienced, and patient.

Balanchine's *Who Cares?* in rehearsal for the Tribute to George Balanchine in 2001. The dancers, from left to right, are Brianna Giles, Craig Sanok, Brianne Bland, Jean Sebastien Couture, Kristine Owen, and Paul Anthony Chambers.

Our tribute to Balanchine was assembled and performed in 2001, a year before the actual centenary of his birth. It was a privilege for our whole team to both create and be included in this celebration. Many of Balanchine's ballets have been a regular part of our summer since 1986, when we first danced *The Four Temperaments*. Since then, we have mounted fourteen different works, some of them several times for succeeding generations, as we believe that any young ballet dancer who enters professional life today will almost certainly dance a work by Balanchine. The Balanchine technique, of course, is an important corollary to his ballets. Here, Chelsea Lindsay and Blair Puente are carefully watched by teacher and coach Victoria Simon.

TEACHERS

Laura Alonso
Anette Amand
Reid Anderson
Gwynne Ashton
Annette av Paul

Patricia Beatty
Michel Boudot
Frank Bourman
Louise Browne
Michael Byars

Ruth Carse
Sonia Chamberlain
James Clouser
Michele-France Cloutier
Shelly Cromie

Bette Davis
Karen du Plessis

Maureen Eastick
Winnifred Edwards
Olga Evreinoff

Julia Farron
Maria Fay
Gladys Forrester
Pat Fraser

Jorge Garcia
Peter George
Choo Chiat Goh
Nana Gollner

Larry Hayden
Alan Hooper

Earl Kraul

David LaHay
Olga Lepeshinskaya
Marquita Lester

Jean McKenzie
Maisie McPhee
Helene Melancon
Margaret Mercier
Jean Louis Morin
David Moroni
Sheila Murray

Pat Neary

Brydon Paige
Nadia Potts

Vicky Simon
Andrea Smith
Raymond Smith
Arnold Spohr
Vicki St. Denys
Joan Sterling

Deirdre Tarrant
Susan Toumine
Mary Tuft

Diane van Schoor
Violette Verdy
Vera Volkova
Eva von Genscy

Virginia Wakelyn

Natalia Zolotova

# Afterword

THE GREAT ACCOMPLISHMENT of The Banff Centre's Summer Dance Program is clear in the preceding pages, which celebrate six decades of exuberant existence. To this day Banff, now under the direction of the distinguished but very approachable Annette av Paul, offers an intense experience where young dancers can fully explore their art. High in the Rocky Mountains and far from the daily routine, there is the time, space, and inspiration necessary for real artistic discovery and growth.

Inspiration begins with the first sight of the impressive mountain environment and continues in the dance world's usual habitats of classroom and stage. At Banff, both these critical workaday milieus support the program participants with superb human and physical resources. Each year, there is a knowledgeable, specialized faculty and full access to The Banff Centre's theatre complex, including the large, well-equipped Eric Harvie Theatre.

This makes possible one of the great benefits of the program's professional division, the chance to spend six weeks as if part of a company. Festival Dance, formed each summer, has a company's usual focus on daily class, rehearsal, and public performance. Banff is not just about getting the gang up on stage and looking good, though. It is also about paying attention to the talented individuals who have been accepted into the program, and assessing their needs and future goals. For some, that might include the discovery that a life on stage is not what they really want after all. For others, Banff can be a launching pad into their first professional job.

Artistic directors from across Canada often talent spot during the shows with which the program concludes but, beyond that, appearing with Festival Dance in a variety of works adds valuable substance to the dancers' résumés. In 2006, when I reviewed the evening for *Dance International* magazine (proof that critics attend, too!), the dancers were coached in Balanchine's 1934 *Serenade* by Victoria Simon, the ballet mistress for the

George Balanchine Trust, and in Brian Macdonald's 1962 *Time Out of Mind*, coached by the master choreographer himself. As well, that year's Clifford E. Lee Choreography Award recipient, Simone Orlando, created a new ballet, *Winter Journey*, with the enthusiastic Banff dancers.

The show served the art form well on many levels. It gave the dancers first-hand experience of important ballets from the past and the chance to participate in the latest Lee Award creation process and premiere. It gave the dance community a close look at today's emerging talent - the dancers, of course, and also choreographer Orlando. And, since we can't take a ballet off the shelf as we can a book, remounting *Time Out of Mind* provided a welcome opportunity to view a significant part of Canada's cultural history. Festival Dance also gave the audience — both insiders and the general public — a splendid evening out.

Clearly, it is more than just the dancers who benefit from the Banff Dance Program, which continues to inspire us all.

Kaija Pepper

"We want you all to enjoy the picnic on Sunday but there are several things to remember. This is a National Park; we must clean up everything before coming back to the Centre. Watch out for the sun, you burn very quickly here in the mountains; and don't even *think* mountain climbing." Seen here are Kelley McKinlay and Gunnlauger Egilsson.

And so it came to pass that the faithful
Were lead into the valley of the river Bow
Where they danced and flourished for many gernerations.

Anon.